ACCESS TO SHAKESPEARE

A Midsummer Night's Dream

A Facing-pages Translation into Contemporary English

Edited by
Jonnie Patricia Mobley, Ph.D.
Drama Department
Cuesta College
San Luis Obispo, California

Lorenz Educational Publishers
P.O. Box 711030, Los Angeles, CA 90071-9625

Cover border taken from the First Folio (1623)

Cover design by Tamada Brown Design, Chicago

Interior design and typesetting by David Corona Design, Dubuque

ISBN: 1-885564-06-6

Library of Congress Card Catalog Card Number: 94-78623
Manufactured in the United States of America.
5 6 7 8 9 0 6 5 4 3 2 1

A Midsummer Night's Dream

Contents

Introduction

This volume of William Shakespeare's *A Midsummer Night's Dream* consists of two versions of the play. The first is the original, based on the *Globe* edition of 1860, which was in turn based on the Folio of 1623. And this, further, was a reprint of a still earlier edition, the Fisher Quarto of 1600. The second version is a translation of the original into contemporary English. In both versions the spelling and punctuation have been updated, and the names of the characters have been spelled out in full for easier reading. Insights from modern scholars have been included in both versions.

The translation of *A Midsummer Night's Dream* is not meant to take the place of the original. Instead, it is an alternative to the notes usually included in modern editions. In many editions these notes interfere with the reading of the play. Whether alongside or below the original text, the notes break the rhythm of reading and frequently force the reader to turn back to an earlier page or jump ahead to a later one. Having a translation that runs parallel to the original, line for line, allows the reader to move easily from Elizabethan to contemporary English and back again. It's simply a better way to introduce Shakespeare.

Also, this translation is suitable for performance, where notes are not available to the audience. Admittedly, a well-directed and well-acted production can do much to clarify Shakespeare's language. And yet, there will be numerous references and lines whose meanings are not accessible to many on a first hearing. What, for instance, does Egeus mean when he accuses Lysander of having "stolen the impression of her fantasy"?

Shakespeare's Language

Shakespeare's language does present problems for modern readers. After all, four centuries separate us from him. During this time words have acquired new meanings or have dropped from the language altogether, and sentence structures have become less fluid. But these are solvable problems.

First of all, most of the words that Shakespeare used are still current. For those words whose meanings have changed and for those words no longer in the language, modern equivalents are found in this translation. For a small number of words—chiefly names of places and mythological characters—a glossary can be found on page 178.

The meaning of words is one problem. The position of words is another. Today, the order of words in declarative sentences is almost fixed. The subject comes first, then the verb, and finally, if there is one, the object. In Shakespeare's time, the order of words, particularly in poetic drama, was more fluid. Shakespeare has Egeus say,

> Full of vexation come I

Whereas we would usually arrange the words in this order,

> I come full of vexation

Later in the play, Lysander tells Hermia about his aunt,

> From Athens is her house remote seven leagues

We would probably say,

> Her house is a remote seven leagues from Athens

This does not mean that Shakespeare never uses words in what we consider today as normal order. As often as not, he does. Here, for instance, are Flute and Quince in conversation,

> FLUTE   What is Thisbe? A wandering knight?
> QUINCE   It is the lady that Pyramus must love.

When Shakespeare does invert the order of words, he does so for a reason or for a variety of reasons—to create a rhythm, to emphasize a word, to achieve a rhyme. Whether a play is in verse, as most of this play is, or in prose, it is still written in sentences. And that means that, despite the order, all the words needed to make complete sentences are there. If you are puzzled by a sentence, first look for the subject and then try rearranging the words in the order that you would normally use. It takes a little practice, but you will be surprised how quickly you acquire the skill.

Shakespeare sometimes separates sentence parts—subject and verb, for example—that would normally be run together. Here are some lines spoken by Titania, describing her friend, the mother of the changeling child,

> Which she, with pretty and with swimming gait
> Following (her womb then rich with my young squire),
> Would imitate...

Between the subject *she* and the verb *would imitate* come two prepositional phrases and a parenthetical comment that interrupt the normal sequence. Again, look for the subject and then the verb and put the two together. You'll find, however, that your rearranged sentence, while clear, is not as rhythmical as Shakespeare's.

Stage Directions

In drama written for the modern stage, the playwright usually provides detailed directions for the actors—how to move and speak, what emotions to convey to an audience. In the plays of Shakespeare, stage directions are sparse. One reason for this could be that Shakespeare was a member and an owner of the company for which he wrote these plays. He was on hand to tell the other actors how to say a line or what gesture to use. Even so, the dialogue itself offers clues to actions or gestures. For example, Lysander and Hermia, in Act Two, become lost in the woods outside Athens and decide to rest there till daybreak. Lysander suggests that they share the same patch of grass,

> One turf shall serve as pillow for us both

Although there is no stage direction indicating that Lysander has moved in close to Hermia, she says,

> Lie further off yet; do not lie so near

In a different scene of the same act, Puck tells the Fairy to make "room" for "here comes Oberon," his master. The Fairy replies "and here my mistress." At this, though again there is no stage direction, Puck and the Fairy probably move aside to allow for the entrance of the king and queen of Fairyland.

Reading the printed play, you have to try to picture the characters and their actions in your mind.

Solo Speeches

There is another difference between the plays of Shakespeare and most modern ones—the solo speeches. These are the asides and the soliloquies in which a character reveals what is on his or her mind. Modern dramatists seem to feel that the solo speech is artificial and unrealistic. Oddly enough, modern novelists frequently use a variety of the solo speech, and some critics feel that this convention has given the novel extra power and depth, allowing it to probe deeply into the motives of its characters. One thing is certain—Shakespeare's plays without the solo speeches would not be as powerful as they are.

A Midsummer Night's Dream

Characters

THESEUS, Duke of Athens

HIPPOLYTA, Queen of the Amazons, betrothed to Theseus

EGEUS, father of Hermia

HERMIA, daughter of Egeus, in love with Lysander

LYSANDER, in love with Hermia

DEMETRIUS, in love with Hermia

HELENA, in love with Demetrius

PHILOSTRATE, master of revels to the duke

PETER QUINCE, a carpenter and "Prologue" in the interlude

NICK BOTTOM, a weaver and "Pyramus" in the interlude

FRANCIS FLUTE, a bellows-mender and "Thisbe" in the interlude

TOM SNOUT, a tinker and the "Wall" in the interlude

ROBIN STARVELING, a tailor and "Moonshine" in the interlude

SNUG, a joiner and the "Lion" in the interlude

OBERON, King of the Fairies

TITANIA, Queen of the Fairies

PUCK (ROBIN GOODFELLOW), Hobgoblin in Oberon's service

PEASEBLOSSOM

COBWEB } Fairies attending

MOTH } on Titania

MUSTARDSEED

Lords and Attendants on Theseus and Hippolyta
Other Fairies attending on Oberon and Titania

1

Act One

Scene 1 [*Athens. The hall in the palace of the duke*]

THESEUS *and* HIPPOLYTA *enter and take their seats, followed by*

PHILOSTRATE *and* ATTENDANTS

THESEUS Now, fair Hippolyta, our nuptial hour

    Draws on apace. Four happy days bring in

    Another moon—but O, methinks how slow

    This old moon wanes! She lingers my desires,

    Like to a step-dame, or a dowager,   5

    Long withering out a young man's revenue.

HIPPOLYTA Four days will quickly steep themselves in night:

    Four nights will quickly dream away the time:

    And then the moon, like to a silver bow

    New-bent in heaven, shall behold the night   10

    Of our solemnities.

THESEUS Go, Philostrate,

    Stir up the Athenian youth to merriments,

    Awake the pert and nimble spirit of mirth,

    Turn melancholy forth to funerals: 15

    The pale companion is not for our pomp.

Exit PHILOSTRATE

    Hippolyta, I wooed thee with my sword,

    And won thy love doing thee injuries:

    But I will wed thee in another key,

    With pomp, with triumph, and with revelling.   20

Act One

Scene 1 [*Athens. The hall in the palace of the duke*]
> THESEUS *and* HIPPOLYTA *enter and take their seats, followed by*
> PHILOSTRATE *and* ATTENDANTS

THESEUS Now, fair Hippolyta, our wedding day
    Draws quickly near: four happy days bring in
    A new moon, but oh, I think how slow
    This old moon fades! It delays my desires,
    Like a stepmother or a widow,   5
    Eating away a young man's inheritance.

HIPPOLYTA Four days will quickly loose themselves in night:
    Four nights will quickly dream away the time:
    And then the crescent moon, like a silver bow
    Newly bent in the heavens, shall watch the night   10
    Of our celebration.

THESEUS Go, Philostrate,
    Stir up the youths of Athens to merriments,
    Awake the pert and nimble spirit of mirth,
    Send melancholy out to funerals;   15
    That pale fellow is not for our feast.

> *Exit* PHILOSTRATE

    Hippolyta, I wooed you with my sword,
    And won your love by warfare:
    But I'll wed you to a different tune,
    With splendor, celebration, and grand display.   20

Enter EGEUS, *with his daughter* HERMIA, *followed by* LYSANDER

and DEMETRIUS

EGEUS   Happy be Theseus, our renowned Duke!

THESEUS   Thanks, good Egeus. What's the news with thee?

EGEUS   Full of vexation come I, with complaint

    Against my child, my daughter Hermia.

    Stand forth, Demetrius. My noble lord,   25

    This man hath my consent to marry her.

    Stand forth, Lysander. And, my gracious Duke,

    This man hath bewitched the bosom of my child.

    Thou, thou, Lysander, thou hast given her rhymes,

    And interchanged love-tokens with my child: 30

    Thou hast by moonlight at her window sung,

    With feigning voice, verses of feigning love:

    And stolen the impression of her fantasy

    With bracelets of thy hair, rings, gauds, conceits,

    Knacks, trifles, nosegays, sweetmeats, messengers   35

    Of strong prevailment in unhardened youth.

    With cunning hast thou filched my daughter's heart,

    Turned her obedience, which is due to me,

    To stubborn harshness.   And, my gracious Duke,

    Be it so she will not here before your Grace   40

    Consent to marry with Demetrius,

    I beg the ancient privilege of Athens:

    As she is mine, I may dispose of her,

    Which shall be either to this gentleman,

    Or to her death; according to our law   45

    Immediately provided in that case.

Enter EGEUS, *pulling along his daughter* HERMIA *by the arm, followed by*
LYSANDER *and* DEMETRIUS

EGEUS Much happiness to you, honored Duke Theseus.

THESEUS Thanks, good Egeus, how are you?

EGEUS I come here with anger to complain

About my child, my daughter Hermia.

Step forward, Demetrius. My noble lord,   25

This man has my consent to marry her.

Step forward, Lysander. And, my gracious Duke,

This man has stolen the heart of my child.

You, you, Lysander, you have given her poems,

And interchanged love tokens with my child,   30

You've serenaded her by moonlight at her window

With a false voice, singing phony love songs

And slyly stamped yourself on her imagination

With bracelets of your hair, rings, toys, fanciful trifles,

Knickknacks, novelties, flowers, candy—strong   35

Persuaders to an inexperienced young girl.

With your cleverness you have stolen my daughter's heart,

Turned the obedience, which she owes me,

To stubborn harshness. And, my gracious Duke,

If she will not here before your Grace   40

Consent to marry Demetrius,

I ask for the ancient privilege of Athens:

As she is mine, I may decide her fate,

Which shall be either to marry Demetrius

Or be put to death, according to the law   45

That applies in such cases.

THESEUS What say you, Hermia? Be advised, fair maid.

    To you your father should be as a god;

    One that composed your beauties; yea and one

    To whom you are but as a form in wax   50

    By him imprinted, and within his power

    To leave the figure or disfigure it.

    Demetrius is a worthy gentleman.

HERMIA So is Lysander.

THESEUS In himself he is;   55

    But in this kind, wanting your father's voice,

    The other must be held the worthier.

HERMIA I would my father looked but with my eyes.

THESEUS Rather your eyes must with his judgment look.

HERMIA I do entreat your Grace to pardon me.   60

    I know not by what power I am made bold;

    Nor how it may concern my modesty

    In such a presence here to plead my thoughts:

    But I beseech your Grace that I may know

    The worst that may befall me in this case   65

    If I refuse to wed Demetrius.

THESEUS Either to die the death, or to abjure

    Forever the society of men.

    Therefore, fair Hermia, question your desires,

    Know of your youth, examine well your blood,   70

    Whether, if you yield not to your father's choice,

THESEUS What do you say, Hermia? Consider this, young lady,
    Your father should be like a god to you;
    He brought you into the world, yes and
    To him you are like a wax figure   50
    He has formed, and it's within his power
    To leave it as it is or to change it.
    Demetrius is a worthy gentleman.

HERMIA So is Lysander.

THESEUS On his own he is;   55
    But in this matter, he lacks your father's consent,
    So the other man must be seen worthier.

HERMIA I wish my father saw him with my eyes.

THESEUS Rather, you must see with your father's eyes.

HERMIA I do beg your Grace to pardon me.   60
    I don't know how I even have the courage to ask,
    Or if it befits my modest position
    To plead my case here before you:
    But I beg your Grace to tell me
    The worst that could happen to me   65
    If I refuse to marry Demetrius.

THESEUS Either to be executed, or to give up
    Forever any contact with men.
    Therefore, fair Hermia, ask yourself what you want,
    Remember how young you are, examine your feelings,   70
    Decide, if you don't accept your father's choice,

You can endure the livery of a nun,
For aye to be in shady cloister mewed,
To live a barren sister all your life,
Chanting faint hymns to the cold fruitless moon.   75
Thrice blessed they that master so their blood,
To undergo such maiden pilgrimage:
But earthlier happy is the rose distilled,
Than that which withering on the virgin thorn
Grows, lives, and dies in single blessedness.   80

HERMIA So will I grow, so live, so die, my lord,
Ere I will yield my virgin patent up
Unto his lordship, whose unwished yoke
My soul consents not to give sovereignty.

THESEUS Take time to pause, and by the next new moon—   85
The sealing-day betwixt my love and me
For everlasting bond of fellowship—
Upon that day either prepare to die
For disobedience to your father's will,
Or else to wed Demetrius, as he would,   90
Or on Diana's altar to protest
For aye austerity and single life.

DEMETRIUS Relent, sweet Hermia—and, Lysander, yield
Thy crazed title to my certain right.

LYSANDER You have her father's love, Demetrius;   95
Let me have Hermia's. Do you marry him.

EGEUS Scornful Lysander! True, he hath my love;
And what is mine my love shall render him.

Whether you can accept the nun's habit,

And live in a shady cloistered convent

As a virgin all your life,

Chanting faint hymns to the cold barren moon. 75

Those who make that choice are three times blessed,

To go through life as virgins:

But the rose picked for perfume has earthly joys

Unknown to the rose that, withering on the bough,

Grows, lives, and dies in single blessedness. 80

HERMIA So will I grow and live and die, my lord,

Before I'll give up my virginity

To a man whose unwanted mastery

My soul cannot consent to accept.

THESEUS Take time to think about it. By the next new moon— 85

The day set for my love and me

To seal our joy in marriage—

On that day either prepare to die

For disobedience to your father's will,

Or to wed Demetrius as he wishes, 90

Or else on the goddess Diana's altar

To vow a single and austere life.

DEMETRIUS Relent, sweet Hermia—and, Lysander, give up

Your flawed claim to my certain right.

LYSANDER You have her father's love, Demetrius, 95

Let me have Hermia's. Go marry him.

EGEUS Scornful Lysander! Yes, he does have my love;

And so I can give him what is mine.

And she is mine, and all my right of her

I do estate unto Demetrius. 100

LYSANDER   I am, my lord, as well derived as he,

As well possessed. My love is more than his;

My fortunes every way as fairly ranked—

If not with vantage—as Demetrius'.

And, which is more than all these boasts can be, 105

I am beloved of beauteous Hermia.

Why should not I then prosecute my right?

Demetrius, I'll avouch it to his head,

Made love to Nedar's daughter, Helena,

And won her soul; and she, sweet lady, dotes, 110

Devoutly dotes, dotes in idolatry,

Upon this spotted and inconstant man.

THESEUS   I must confess that I have heard so much:

And with Demetrius thought to have spoke thereof;

But, being over-full of self-affairs, 115

My mind did lose it. [*He rises*] But Demetrius come,

And come Egeus, you shall go with me.

I have some private schooling for you both.

For you, fair Hermia, look to arm yourself

To fit your fancies to your father's will; 120

Or else the law of Athens yields you up

(Which by no means we may extenuate)

To death or to a vow of single life.

Come, my Hippolyta. What cheer, my love?

Demetrius and Egeus, go along: 125

I must employ you in some business

Hermia is mine and, as is my right,

I give her to Demetrius.   100

LYSANDER My lord, I am from as good a family as he,

I'm as wealthy. My love is stronger than his:

My prospects are at least equal—

If not even better—than Demetrius'.

And, which means more than any of these things,   105

I am loved by beautiful Hermia.

Why shouldn't I then put forth my case?

Demetrius, I'll say it to his face,

Made love to Nedar's daughter, Helena,

And won her heart; and she, sweet lady, dotes,   110

Devoutly dotes, dotes in idolatry,

Upon this wicked and faithless man.

THESEUS I must confess that I have heard that too

And thought to speak to Demetrius about it,

But, being preoccupied with my own concerns,   115

I forgot about it. [He rises] But come, Demetrius,

And come, Egeus, you shall go with me:

I have some private advice for you both.

As for you, fair Hermia, decide to adapt yourself

To fit your wishes to your father's will;   120

Or else the law of Athens condemns you

(And we will not modify it)

To death or to a vow of single life.

Come, my Hippolyta. Cheer up, my love.

Demetrius and Egeus, come along: 125

I have some errands for you

Against our nuptial, and confer with you

Of something nearly that concerns yourselves.

EGEUS With duty and desire we follow you.

Exit save HERMIA *and* LYSANDER

LYSANDER How now, my love? Why is your cheek so pale? 130

How chance the roses there do fade so fast?

HERMIA Belike for want of rain, which I could well

Beteem them from the tempest of my eyes.

LYSANDER Ay me! For aught that I could ever read,

Could ever hear by tale or history, 135

The course of true love never did run smooth;

But, either it was different in blood—

HERMIA O cross! Too high to be enthralled to low.

LYSANDER Or else misgraffed in respect of years—

HERMIA O spite! Too old to be engaged to young. 140

LYSANDER Or else it stood upon the choice of friends—

HERMIA O hell! To choose love by another's eyes!

LYSANDER Or, if there were a sympathy in choice,

War, death, or sickness did lay siege to it,

Making it momentary as a sound, 145

Swift as a shadow, short as any dream,

Brief as the lightning in the collied night

That, in a spleen, unfolds both heaven and earth;

And ere a man hath power to say "Behold!"

The jaws of darkness do devour it up: 150

So quick bright things come to confusion.

Concerning my wedding, and want to consult you

About some personal matters.

EGEUS It's our duty and pleasure to obey you.

Exit all but HERMIA *and* LYSANDER

LYSANDER What's wrong, my love? Why are you so pale?   130

Why do the roses in your cheeks fade so quickly?

HERMIA Maybe for lack of rain, which I could well

Provide them from the storm of tears in my eyes.

LYSANDER Oh yes. From all that I've read

Or ever heard in stories or from history   135

The course of true love never did run smooth;

But it was either a difference in class—

HERMIA What a trial! Too upper-class to love someone lower.

LYSANDER Or else too far apart in age—

HERMIA Oh spite! Too old to be engaged to someone younger.   140

LYSANDER Or else one's relatives object—

HERMIA What hell! To have to accept what others choose.

LYSANDER Or, even if the choice pleased everyone,

War, death, or sickness interfered with it

And made it as momentary as a sound,   145

Swift as a shadow, short as any dream,

Brief as the lightning in the coal-black night

That, in a fit, lights up both heaven and earth;

And before you can say "Look at that!"

The darkness swallows it up: 150

So quickly are bright things destroyed.

HERMIA If then true lovers have been ever crossed,

    It stands as an edict in destiny:

    Then let us teach our trial patience,

    Because it is a customary cross,   155

    As due to love as thoughts, and dreams, and sighs,

    Wishes, and tears—poor Fancy's followers.

LYSANDER A good persuasion. Therefore hear me, Hermia:

    I have a widow aunt, a dowager

    Of great revenue, and she hath no child.   160

    From Athens is her house remote seven leagues;

    And she respects me as her only son.

    There, gentle Hermia, may I marry thee;

    And to that place the sharp Athenian law

    Cannot pursue us. If thou lovest me, then,   165

    Steal forth thy father's house tomorrow night;

    And in the wood, a league without the town,

    Where I did meet thee once with Helena,

    To do observance to a morn of May,

    There will I stay for thee.   170

HERMIA My good Lysander,

    I swear to thee by Cupid's strongest bow,

    By his best arrow with the golden head,

    By the simplicity of Venus' doves,

    By that which knitteth souls and prospers loves,   175

    And by that fire which burned the Carthage queen,

    When the false Trojan under sail was seen,

    By all the vows that ever men have broke—

HERMIA   Well, since true lovers have always been thwarted,
    It must be a law of fate;
    Then, let us show patience in our trials,
    Because this always happens to lovers,   155
    As much a part of love as thoughts, and dreams, and sighs,
    Wishes, and tears; poor love's followers.

LYSANDER   That's a good argument. Therefore listen, Hermia:
    I have an elderly widowed aunt,
    Very wealthy, and she has no children.   160
    She lives about twenty miles from Athens,
    And she considers me her only son.
    There, gentle Hermia, I will marry you;
    When we're there the cruel law of Athens
    Cannot touch us. If you love me, then   165
    Sneak out of your father's house tomorrow night;
    And in the wood, about three miles from town,
    Where I met you once with Helena,
    To celebrate the first of May,
    There I'll wait to meet you.   170

HERMIA   My dear Lysander,
    I swear to you by Cupid's strongest bow,
    By his best arrow with the golden tip,
    By the gentleness of Venus' doves,
    By the belt of Venus that joins souls and helps loves,   175
    And by the fire that destroyed the deserted Dido
    When the faithless Aeneas sailed away,
    By all the vows that men have ever broke—

In number more than ever women spoke—
In the same place thou hast appointed me, 180
Tomorrow truly will I meet with thee.

LYSANDER Keep promise, love. Look, here comes Helena.

Enter HELENA

HERMIA God speed, fair Helena! Whither away?

HELENA Call you me fair? That "fair" again unsay.
Demetrius loves your fair. O happy fair! 185
Your eyes are lodestars, and your tongue's sweet air
More tuneable than lark to shepherd's ear,
When wheat is green, when hawthorn buds appear.
Sickness is catching. O, were favor so,
Yours would I catch, fair Hermia, ere I go! 190
My ear should catch your voice, my eye your eye,
My tongue should catch your tongue's sweet melody.
Were the world mine, Demetrius being bated,
The rest I'd give to be to you translated.
O, teach me how you look, and with what art 195
You sway the motion of Demetrius' heart.

HERMIA I frown upon him, yet he loves me still.

HELENA O that your frowns would teach my smiles
such skill!

HERMIA I give him curses, yet he gives me love. 200

HELENA O that my prayers could such affection move!

HERMIA The more I hate, the more he follows me.

HELENA The more I love, the more he hateth me.

More in number than women ever spoke—

In the place you've described to me,   180

There tomorrow me you'll see.

LYSANDER Keep your promise, love. Look, here comes Helena.

Enter HELENA

HERMIA Good day, fair Helena. Are you going away?

HELENA Did you call me fair? That "fair" again unsay.

Demetrius loves your fair. Oh, happy fair!   185

Your eyes are guiding stars, your tongue's sweet air

Is more musical than a lark to a shepherd's ear,

When wheat is green, and hawthorn buds appear.

Sickness is catching. If I were favored so,

I would catch what you have, fair Hermia, before I go!   190

My ear should catch your voice, my eye your eye,

My tongue should catch your tongue's sweet melody

If the world were mine, I'd hold to Demetrius true,

And give everything else to be changed into you.

Oh, teach me how you look, and with what art   195

You capture the rhythm of Demetrius' heart.

HERMIA I frown at him, but he loves me still.

HELENA Oh, that your frowns would teach my smiles
such skill!

HERMIA I give him curses, yet he gives me love.   200

HELENA Oh, that my prayers could such affection move.

HERMIA The more I hate him, the more he follows me.

HELENA The more I love him, the more he hates me.

HERMIA His folly, Helena, is no fault of mine.

HELENA None, but your beauty; would that fault were mine   205

HERMIA Take comfort. He no more shall see my face;

    Lysander and myself will fly this place.

    Before the time I did Lysander see,

    Seemed Athens as a paradise to me:

    O then, what graces in my love do dwell,   210

    That he hath turned a heaven unto a hell!

LYSANDER Helen, to you our minds we will unfold:

    Tomorrow night, when Phoebe doth behold

    Her silver visage in the wat'ry glass,

    Decking with liquid pearl the bladed grass—   215

    A time that lovers' flights doth still conceal—

    Through Athens' gates have we devised to steal.

HERMIA And in the wood, where often you and I

    Upon faint primrose beds were wont to lie,

    Emptying our blossoms of their counsel sweet   220

    There my Lysander and myself shall meet,

    And thence from Athens turn away our eyes

    To seek new friends and stranger companies.

    Farewell, sweet playfellow. Pray thou for us:

    And good luck grant thee thy Demetrius!   225

    Keep word, Lysander. We must starve our sight

    From lovers' food till morrow deep midnight.

LYSANDER I will, my Hermia.

Exit HERMIA

    Helena, adieu!

    As you on him, Demetrius dote on you!   230

Exit LYSANDER

HELENA How happy some o'er other some can be!

HERMIA   Helena, his foolishness is no fault of mine.

HELENA   None, but your beauty. I wish that fault were mine.   205

HERMIA   Take comfort. He shall no more see my face;

    Lysander and I will be leaving this place.

    Before the time I did Lysander see,

    Athens seemed like a paradise to me:

    Oh, then what graces in my love do dwell,   210

    That he makes this heaven seem like a hell!

LYSANDER   Helena, we will now our secret unfold:

    Tomorrow night, when the moon can behold

    Her silver reflection in the watery glass,

    Covering with liquid pearl the blades of grass—   215

    A time lovers' flights would be concealed from all—

    We've decided to sneak out through Athens' wall.

HERMIA   And in the wood, where often you and I

    Upon the pale primrose beds liked to lie

    Telling each other our heart's secrets sweet   220

    There Lysander and I plan to meet,

    And away from Athens turn our eyes,

    To find new friends and different companies.

    Farewell, dear playmate: Pray for us,

    And may good luck help you win Demetrius!   225

    Keep your word, Lysander. We must starve our sight

    Of each other till we meet tomorrow at midnight.

LYSANDER   I will, my Hermia.

Exit HERMIA

    Goodbye, Helena true,

    As you love Demetrius, may he love you!   230

Exit LYSANDER

HELENA   How much happier some are than others can be!

Through Athens I am thought as fair as she,
But what of that? Demetrius thinks not so;
He will not know what all but he do know.
And as he errs, doting on Hermia's eyes,   235
So I, admiring of his qualities.
Things base and vile, holding no quantity,
Love can transpose to form and dignity.
Love looks not with the eyes, but with the mind:
And therefore is winged Cupid painted blind.   240
Nor hath Love's mind of any judgment taste:
Wings and no eyes figure unheedy haste.
And therefore is Love said to be a child
Because in choice he is so oft beguiled.
As waggish boys in game themselves forswear,   245
So the boy Love is perjured everywhere.
For ere Demetrius looked on Hermia's eyne,
He hailed down oaths that he was only mine,
And when this hail some heat from Hermia felt
So he dissolved, and show'rs of oaths did melt.   250
I will go tell him of fair Hermia's flight.
Then to the wood will he tomorrow night
Pursue her; and for this intelligence,
If I have thanks, it is a dear expense.
But herein mean I to enrich my pain,   255
To have his sight thither and back again.

Exit

Through Athens I'm thought as fair as she.
But what of that? Demetrius doesn't think so:
He won't accept what all but he must know,
And as he errs, doting on Hermia's eyes,   235
So I err, admiring all his qualities.
Things low and vile, with no quality,
Are changed by Love in form and dignity.
Love looks not with the eyes, but with the mind:
That's why winged Cupid is pictured blind.   240
Nor does Love's mind have any taste;
His wings and blindfold suggest reckless haste.
And that's why Love is said to be a child:
Because in choice he's so often beguiled.
As joking boys in a game do swear,   245
The boy Love is perjured everywhere.
Before Demetrius found Hermia so fine,
He hailed down oaths that he was mine.
But when this "hail" some heat from Hermia felt,
So he dissolved and all his oaths did melt.   250
I will go tell him of fair Hermia's flight.
Then he'll to the woods tomorrow night
And pursue her; and for this precious news,
He'll give me nothing I can use.
But at least it will somewhat dull my pain   255
To see and meet with him again.

Exits

Scene 2 [*Athens. A room in the cottage of Peter Quince*]

    Enter QUINCE, BOTTOM, SNUG, FLUTE, SNOUT, *and* STARVELING

QUINCE Is all our company here?

BOTTOM You were best to call them generally, man by
    man, according to the scrip.

QUINCE Here is the scroll of every man's name, which
    is thought fit, through all Athens, to play in our interlude   5
    before the Duke and the Duchess, on his wedding day at night.

BOTTOM First, good Peter Quince, say what the play
    treats on; then read the names of the actors; and so
    grow to a point.

QUINCE Marry, our play is "The Most Lamentable   10
    Comedy, and Most Cruel Death of Pyramus and Thisbe."

BOTTOM A very good piece of work, I assure you, and a
    merry. Now, good Peter Quince, call forth your actors
    by the scroll. Masters, spread yourselves.

QUINCE Answer, as I call you. Nick Bottom, the weaver?   15

BOTTOM Ready. Name what part I am for, and proceed.

QUINCE You, Nick Bottom, are set down for Pyramus.

BOTTOM What is Pyramus? A lover, or a tyrant?

QUINCE A lover that kills himself, most gallant for love.

BOTTOM That will ask some tears in the true performing   20
    of it. If I do it, let the audience look to their eyes!
    I will move storms; I will condole in some measure.

Scene 2 [*Athens. A room in the cottage of Peter Quince*]

Enter QUINCE, BOTTOM, SNUG, FLUTE, SNOUT, *and* STARVELING

QUINCE Is everybody here?

BOTTOM You'd better call each man, one by one, according
    to the list.

QUINCE Here's a list of every man's name who
    throughout all Athens is thought fit to be in our play   5
    for the Duke and Duchess, on their wedding day, at night.

BOTTOM First, good Peter Quince, say what the play
    is about; then read the names of the actors; and so
    get to the end of the sentence.

QUINCE All right, our play is "The Most Lamentable   10
    Comedy and Most Cruel Death of Pyramus and Thisbe."

BOTTOM A very good piece of work, I assure you, and a
    merry one. Now, good Peter Quince, call out your actors
    from the list. Gentlemen, sit down.

QUINCE Answer when I call you. Nick Bottom, the weaver?   15

BOTTOM Ready. Say what part I play and then go on.

QUINCE You, Nick Bottom, will play Pyramus.

BOTTOM What is Pyramus? A lover or a dictator?

QUINCE A lover who kills himself, most gallantly for love.

BOTTOM That will require me to cry to perform it well.   20
    If I do it, the audience will cry too:
    I will storm around: I will lament at length.

To the rest—yet my chief humor is for a tyrant.
I could play Ercles rarely, or a part to tear a cat in, to
make all split.   25

     "The raging rocks

     And shivering shocks

     Shall break the locks

       Of prison gates,

     And Phibbus' car   30

     Shall shine from far

     And make and mar

       The foolish Fates."

This was lofty. Now name the rest of the players. This
is Ercles' vein, a tyrant's vein. A lover is more condoling.   35

QUINCE Francis Flute, the bellows-mender?

FLUTE Here, Peter Quince.

QUINCE Flute, you must take Thisbe on you.

FLUTE What is Thisbe? A wandering knight?

QUINCE It is the lady that Pyramus must love.   40

FLUTE Nay, faith, let not me play a woman. I have a
beard coming.

QUINCE That's all one. You shall play it in a mask, and
you may speak as small as you will.

BOTTOM An I may hide my face, let me play Thisbe too.   45
I'll speak in a monstrous little voice. "Thisne, Thisne!"
"Ah, Pyramus, my lover dear! Thy Thisbe dear, and
lady dear."

QUINCE No, no, you must play Pyramus; and Flute,
you Thisbe.   50

Well, go on to the others—yet, I'd rather do a dictator.

I could play Hercules well, or a part with violent gestures,

to tear everything apart.   25

     "The raging rocks

     And shivering shocks

     Shall break the locks

       Of prison gates,

     And Phoebus' car   30

     Shall shine from far

     And make and mar

       The foolish Fates."

That was lofty. Now name the rest of the players. This

is Hercules' tone, a dictator's tone. A lover's softer.   35

QUINCE Francis Flute, the bellows-mender?

FLUTE Here, Peter Quince.

QUINCE Flute, you must take the part of Thisbe.

FLUTE What is Thisbe, a wandering knight?

QUINCE It's the lady that Pyramus loves.   40

FLUTE No, please, don't ask me to play a woman. I have a

    beard coming in.

QUINCE That's all right. You can play it in a mask, and

    you must speak as delicately as you can.

BOTTOM I could hide my face, let me play Thisbe too.   45

    I'll speak in a monstrous little voice. "Thisne, Thisne."

    "Ah, Pyramus, my lover dear, your Thisbe dear, and

    lady dear."

QUINCE No, no, you must play Pyramus; and Flute,

    you must play Thisbe.   50

BOTTOM Well, proceed.

QUINCE Robin Starveling, the tailor?

STARVELING Here, Peter Quince.

QUINCE Robin Starveling, you must play Thisbe's
    mother. Tom Snout, the tinker?   55

SNOUT Here, Peter Quince.

QUINCE You, Pyramus' father; myself, Thisbe's father;
    Snug, the joiner, you the lion's part; and I hope here
    is a play fitted.

SNUG Have you the lion's part written? Pray you, if   60
    it be, give it me; for I am slow of study.

QUINCE You may do it extempore; for it is nothing but
    roaring.

BOTTOM Let me play the lion too. I will roar that I will
    do any man's heart good to hear me. I will roar that   65
    I will make the Duke say, "Let him roar again, let him
    roar again."

QUINCE An you should do it too terribly, you would
    fright the Duchess and the ladies that they would shriek;
    and that were enough to hang us all.   70

ALL That would hang us, every mother's son.

BOTTOM I grant you, friends, if you should fright the
    ladies out of their wits, they would have no more
    discretion but to hang us. But I will aggravate my voice
    so, that I will roar you as gently as a sucking dove.   75
    I will roar you an 'twere any nightingale.

QUINCE You can play no part but Pyramus; for Pyramus
    is a sweet-faced man; a proper man as one shall see in

BOTTOM Well, proceed.

QUINCE Robin Starveling, the tailor?

STARVELING Here, Peter Quince.

QUINCE Robin Starveling, you must play Thisbe's
    mother. Tom Snout, the tinker?   55

SNOUT Here, Peter Quince.

QUINCE You, Pyramus' father; myself, Thisbe's father;
    Snug, the joiner, you the lion's part; and I hope this
    is a play to fit the occasion.

SNUG Have you the lion's part written down? If so, please   60
    give it to me as I'm slow to learn.

QUINCE You can improvise it, it's nothing but
    roaring.

BOTTOM Let me play the lion, too. I will roar so that it will
    please anyone to hear me. I will roar so that   65
    the Duke will say, "Let him roar again, let him
    roar again."

QUINCE And you would do it too terribly, so that you would
    frighten the Duchess and the ladies, and they would shriek;
    And that would be enough to hang us all.   70

ALL That would hang us, every mother's son.

BOTTOM I agree, friends, if you should frighten the
    ladies out of their wits, they would have no choice
    but to hang us. But I will aggravate my voice
    so, that I will roar as gently as a baby dove.   75
    I will roar soft as any nightingale.

QUINCE You can play no part but Pyramus; for Pyramus
    is a sweet-faced man; as proper a man as one could see in

a summer's day; a most lovely, gentleman-like man.

Therefore you must needs play Pyramus.   80

BOTTOM Well, I will undertake it. What beard were

I best to play it in?

QUINCE Why, what you will.

BOTTOM I will discharge it in either your straw color

beard, your orange-tawny beard, your purple-in-grain   85

beard, or your French-crown-color beard, your perfect

yellow.

QUINCE Some of your French crowns have no hair at

all; and then you will play barefaced! But, masters, here

are your parts, and I am to entreat you, request you, and desire   90

you, to con them by tomorrow night, and meet me in

the palace wood, a mile without the town, by moonlight.

There will we rehearse; for if we meet in the city,

we shall be dogged with company, and our devices known.

In the meantime I will draw a bill of properties, such as   95

our play wants. I pray you, fail me not.

BOTTOM We will meet, and there we may rehearse most

obscenely and courageously. Take pains, be perfect.

Adieu.

QUINCE At the Duke's oak we meet.   100

BOTTOM Enough; hold or cut bow-strings.

Exeunt

a summer's day; a most lovely, gentlemanlike man.

Therefore you must play Pyramus. 80

BOTTOM Well, I will take it on. What beard should
I play it in?

QUINCE Why, whatever you like.

BOTTOM I'll play it then in either your straw-color
beard, your orange-tawny beard, your permanent-dye- 85
purple beard, or your French-crown-color beard, your
perfect yellow.

QUINCE Some of your French crowns have no hair at
all, and then you will play barefaced. Gentlemen, here
are your parts, and I beg you, request you, and desire 90
you, to learn them by tomorrow night and meet me in
the palace wood, a mile outside the town, by moonlight.
There we'll rehearse, for if we meet in the city, we shall
be bothered by an audience who'll learn all our plans.
In the meantime, I'll draw up a list of the props our play 95
needs. I beg you, don't fail me.

BOTTOM We will meet, and there we will rehearse most
obscenely and courageously. Make an effort, be perfect,
goodbye.

QUINCE We'll meet at the Duke's oak. 100

BOTTOM Enough! Be there or you're out!

All Exit

Act Two

Scene 1 [*The palace wood, a league from Athens*]

Enter PUCK (ROBIN GOODFELLOW) *and a* FAIRY

PUCK How now, spirit! Whither wander you?

FAIRY Over hill, over dale,
    Thorough bush, thorough briar,
Over park, over pale,
    Thorough flood, thorough fire,   5
I do wander everywhere,
Swifter than the moon's sphere,
And I serve the Fairy Queen,
To dew her orbs upon the green.
The cowslips tall her pensioners be;   10
In their gold coats spots you see;
Those be rubies, fairy favors:
In those freckles live their savors.
I must go seek some dewdrops here,
And hang a pearl in every cowslip's ear.   15
Farewell, thou lob of spirits: I'll be gone.
Our queen and all her elves come here anon.

PUCK The King doth keep his revels here tonight.
Take heed the Queen come not within his sight,
For Oberon is passing fell and wrath,   20
Because that she as her attendant hath
A lovely boy, stolen from an Indian king.
She never had so sweet a changeling,

Act Two

Scene 1 [*The palace wood, a league from Athens*]

Enter PUCK (ROBIN GOODFELLOW) *and a* FAIRY

PUCK Hey, spirit! Where are you going?

FAIRY   Over hill, over dale,
                Through bush, through briar,
                Over park, over rail,
                    Through flood, through fire,   5
                I do wander everywhere,
                Swifter than the moon's sphere,
                And I serve the Fairy Queen,
                By dewing fairy rings upon the green.
                The tall cowslips her bodyguards be;   10
                In their gold coats the spots you see
                Are rubies, fairy presents;
                In those spots live their sweet scents.
        I must go seek some dewdrops here,
        And hang a pearl in every cowslip's ear.   15
        Farewell, you clumsy clown; I'll disappear.
        Our Queen and all her elves will soon be here.

PUCK The King will have his frolics here tonight.
        Be sure the Queen doesn't come within his sight.
        For Oberon is both fierce and wrathful   20
        That she has as an attendant faithful—
        A lovely boy, stolen from an Indian king.
        She never had so sweet a changeling.

31

And jealous Oberon would have the child
Knight of his train, to trace the forests wild;   25
But she, perforce, withholds the loved boy,
Crowns him with flowers, and makes him all her joy.
And now they never meet in grove or green,
By fountain clear, or spangled starlight sheen,
But they do square, that all their elves, for fear,   30
Creep into acorn cups and hide them there.

FAIRY Either I mistake your shape and making quite
    Or else you are that shrewd and knavish sprite
    Called Robin Goodfellow. Are not you he
    That frights the maidens of the villagery,   35
    Skim milk, and sometimes labor in the quern,
    And bootless make the breathless housewife churn,
    And sometime make the drink to bear no barm,
    Mislead night-wanderers, laughing at their harm?
    Those that "Hobgoblin" call you and "Sweet Puck,"   40
    You do their work, and they shall have good luck.
    Are not you he?

PUCK Thou speakest aright;
    I am that merry wanderer of the night.
    I jest to Oberon, and make him smile   45
    When I a fat and bean-fed horse beguile,
    Neighing in likeness of a filly foal;
    And sometime lurk I in a gossip's bowl
    In very likeness of a roasted crab,
    And, when she drinks, against her lips I bob,   50
    And on her withered dewlap pour the ale.
    The wisest aunt, telling the saddest tale,

And jealous Oberon now wants the child
As his own attendant, to range the forest wild.   25
But she insists on keeping the boy,
Crowns him with flowers; he's her joy.
So now they never meet in grove or green,
By fountain clear, or spangled starlight sheen,
Without a fight—and all their elves, for fear,   30
Creep into acorn cups and hide in there.

FAIRY   Either I mistake your shape and features quite
Or else you are that clever roguish sprite
Called Robin Goodfellow. Are you not he
Who frightens maidens in the villagery?   35
You steal the cream and work the corn mill
So the breathless housewife labors for nil,
And sometimes you make sure the beer yeast fails,
Mislead night wanderers and laugh at their wails?
Some call you "Hobgoblin" and "Sweet Puck,"   40
For you do their work and bring them good luck.
Aren't you he?

PUCK   You have it right;
I am that merry wanderer of the night.
I joke with Oberon and make him smile   45
When I a fat and bean-fed horse beguile,
By neighing like a young female foal;
And sometimes I hide in a gossips's bowl,
In the very likeness of a roasted apple,
And when she drinks with it she'll grapple,   50
And on her withered chin spill the ale.
The wisest aunt telling the saddest tale

Sometime for three-foot stool mistaketh me,
Then slip I from her bum. Down topples she,
And "tailor" cries, and falls into a cough;   55
And then the whole choir hold their hips and laugh,
And waxen in their mirth, and neeze, and swear
A merrier hour was never wasted there.
But room, Fairy! Here comes Oberon.

FAIRY And here my mistress. Would that he were gone!   60

     Enter OBERON *with his train and* TITANIA *with hers*

OBERON Ill met by moonlight, proud Titania.

TITANIA What, jealous Oberon! Fairies, skip hence.
I have forsworn his bed and company.

OBERON Tarry, rash wanton! Am not I thy lord?

TITANIA Then I must be thy lady. But I know   65
When thou hast stolen away from Fairyland,
And in the shape of Corin sat all day,
Playing on pipes of corn, and versing love
To amorous Phillida. Why art thou here,
Come from the farthest steep of India,   70
But that, forsooth, the bouncing Amazon,
Your buskined mistress and your warrior love,
To Theseus must be wedded, and you come
To give their bed joy and prosperity?

OBERON How canst thou thus for shame, Titania,   75
Glance at my credit with Hippolyta,
Knowing I know thy love to Theseus?
Didst thou not lead him through the glimmering night

Sometimes for a three-legged stool mistakes me.

I slip out from her bottom and down tumbles she,

And "traitor" shouts and starts to cough;   55

And then the whole choir hold their sides and laugh.

As their mirth grows, they sneeze and swear

There never was a merrier hour spent there.

But make room, Fairy, here comes Oberon.

FAIRY   And here's my mistress. I wish he were gone!   60

    Enter OBERON *with his attendants and* TITANIA *with hers*

OBERON   We're ill met by moonlight, proud Titania.

TITANIA   What, jealous Oberon! Fairies skip away—

I am avoiding his bed and company.

OBERON   Wait, hasty wench. Aren't I your husband?

TITANIA   Then I must be your wife. But I know   65

When you have stolen away from Fairyland,

And disguised as a shepherd, sat all day,

Playing on reed pipes and reciting love poems

To a loving shepherdess. Why are you here,

All the way from the mountains of India?   70

It must be because the bouncing Amazon,

Your long-limbed mistress, your warrior love,

Is to be married to Theseus, and you're here

To bless their bed with joy and prosperity.

OBERON   Shame on you, how can you say this, Titania,   75

And stain my reputation by naming Hippolyta.

I know how much you love Theseus.

Didn't you lead him through the glimmering night

From Perigouna, whom he ravished?
And make him with fair Aegles break his faith,   80
With Ariadne and Antiopa?
TITANIA   These are the forgeries of jealousy:
And never, since the middle summer's spring,
Met we on hill, in dale, forest, or mead,
By paved fountain, or by rushy brook,   85
Or in the beached margent of the sea,
To dance our ringlets to the whistling wind,
But with thy brawls thou hast disturbed our sport.
Therefore the winds, piping to us in vain,
As in revenge, have sucked up from the sea   90
Contagious fogs, which, falling in the land,
Hath every pelting river made so proud
That they have overborne their continents.
The ox hath therefore stretched his yoke in vain,
The ploughman lost his sweat, and the green corn   95
Hath rotted ere his youth attained a beard;
The fold stands empty in the drowned field,
And crows are fatted with the murrain flock.
The nine-men's-morris is filled up with mud,
And the quaint mazes in the wanton green,   100
For lack of tread, are indistinguishable.
The human mortals want their winter cheer.
No night is now with hymn or carol blessed.
Therefore the moon, the governess of floods,
Pale in her anger, washes all the air,   105
That rheumatic diseases do abound.

To escape Perigenia whom he had seduced?

And make him break faith with fair Aegle,   80

As well as with Ariadne and Antiope?

TITANIA   These are the inventions of jealousy:

And never, since the start of midsummer,

Have we met on hill, in dale, forest, or meadow,

By paved fountain, or by weedy brook,   85

Or on the beachy seashore,

To dance our rings in the whistling wind,

But you have disturbed our sport with your brawls.

Therefore the winds, singing to us in vain,

In revenge have drawn up from the sea   90

Contagious fogs; which have fallen on the lands

And swelled every little river

Till they have overflowed their banks.

The ox has strained his neck in vain,

The plowman sweated for nothing, and the green corn   95

Has rotted before it was ready to eat.

Sheepfolds stand empty in the drowned fields,

And the crows grow fat on disease-killed cattle;

The morris board is filled up with mud,

And the charming paths through the fields, from lack   100

Of use, no longer show up against the grass.

Human beings long for their winter cheer.

No hymns or carols fill the night air.

Therefore the moon, the ruler of tides,

Pale in her anger, brings constant rain,   105

That causes rheumatic diseases to spread.

And thorough this distemperature we see
The seasons alter: Hoary-headed frosts
Fall in the fresh lap of the crimson rose,
And on old Hiems' thin and icy crown   110
An odorous chaplet of sweet summer buds
Is, as in mockery, set. The spring, the summer,
The childing autumn, angry winter, change
Their wonted liveries, and the mazed world,
By their increase, now knows not which is which.   115
And this same progeny of evils comes
From our debate, from our dissension:
We are their parents and original.

OBERON Do you amend it then. It lies in you.
Why should Titania cross her Oberon?   120
I do but beg a little changeling boy,
To be my henchman.

TITANIA Set your heart at rest,
The Fairyland buys not the child of me.
His mother was a vot'ress of my order,   125
And in the spiced Indian air by night
Full often hath she gossiped by my side
And sat with me on Neptune's yellow sands,
Marking the embarked traders on the flood,
When we have laughed to see the sails conceive   130
And grow big-bellied with the wanton wind;
Which she, with pretty and with swimming gait
Following (her womb then rich with my young squire),
Would imitate, and sail upon the land

Because of this bad weather, we see
The seasons alter: Chilly frosts
Fall upon the petals of the crimson rose,
And on winter's thin and icy crown,   110
A scented wreath of sweet summer buds
Is, as if in mockery, set. The spring, the summer,
The scolding autumn, angry winter, change
Their usual uniforms, and the amazed world
Now doesn't know whether to expect frost or flowers.   115
And all these offspring of evil come
From our debate, from our quarrel:
We are their parents and their origin.

OBERON Well, you fix it then; it's up to you.
Why should Titania cross her Oberon?   120
All I ask for is a little changeling boy,
To be my page.

TITANIA Set your heart at rest,
All of Fairyland cannot buy the boy from me.
His mother was a devotee of mine,   125
And in the spiced Indian air, by night
Often sat and gossiped by my side;
And watched with me on the ocean's yellow sands,
The ships of traders on the flood tide;
Where we laughed to see the sails conceive   130
And grow big-bellied with the playful wind,
Which she—with a pretty, gliding walk
Following, her womb then rich with the young boy—
Would imitate, and sail upon the land,

To fetch me trifles, and return again, 135
As from a voyage, rich with merchandise.
But she, being mortal, of that boy did die,
And for her sake do I rear up her boy;
And for her sake I will not part with him.

OBERON How long within this wood intend you stay? 140

TITANIA Perchance till after Theseus' wedding day.
If you will patiently dance in our round
And see our moonlight revels, go with us.
If not, shun me, and I will spare your haunts.

OBERON Give me that boy, and I will go with thee. 145

TITANIA Not for thy fairy kingdom! Fairies, away!
We shall chide downright, if I longer stay.

Exit TITANIA *with her train*

OBERON Well, go thy way. Thou shalt not from this grove
Till I torment thee for this injury.
My gentle Puck, come hither. Thou rememb'rest 150
Since once I sat upon a promontory
And heard a mermaid on a dolphin's back
Uttering such dulcet and harmonious breath
That the rude sea grew civil at her song,
And certain stars shot madly from their spheres 155
To hear the sea-maid's music.

PUCK I remember.

OBERON That very time I saw—but thou couldst not—
Flying between the cold moon and the earth,
Cupid all armed. A certain aim he took 160

To fetch me trifles, and return again,   135

As from a voyage, rich with merchandise.

But she, being mortal, died in childbirth;

And for her sake, I raise her boy;

And for her sake, I will not part with him.

OBERON   How long in this wood will you stay?   140

TITANIA   Maybe till after Theseus' wedding day.

If you'll be content to dance in our ring

And see our moonlight revels, go with us.

If not, keep away from me, and I'll avoid your haunts.

OBERON   Give me the boy, and I'll leave with you.   145

TITANIA   Not for your whole kingdom. Fairies, away!

We'll surely fight if I longer stay.

Exit TITANIA *with her attendants*

OBERON   Well, go your way, but you'll not leave this grove

Till I pay you back for this injury.

My gentle Puck, come here. You remember   150

That time I sat upon a promontory,

And heard a mermaid on a dolphin's back

Singing with such a sweet and harmonious voice

That the wild sea grew calm at her song,

And certain stars shot madly from their spheres   155

To hear the sea-maid's music.

PUCK   I remember.

OBERON   At that time I saw—though you could not—

Flying between cold moon and earth,

Cupid all armed; he took accurate aim   160

At a fair vestal, throned by the west,

And loosed his love-shaft smartly form his bow,

As it should pierce a hundred thousand hearts.

But I might see young Cupid's fiery shaft

Quenched in the chaste beams of the wat'ry moon,   165

And the imperial vot'ress passed on,

In maiden meditation, fancy-free.

Yet marked I where the bolt of Cupid fell.

It fell upon a little western flower,

Before, milk-white; now purple with love's wound,   170

And maidens call it "love-in-idleness."

Fetch me that flower; the herb I showed thee once.

The juice of it on sleeping eyelids laid

Will make or man or woman madly dote

Upon the next live creature that it sees.   175

Fetch me this herb, and be thou here again

Ere the leviathan can swim a league.

PUCK I'll put a girdle round about the earth

In forty minutes.

Exit PUCK

OBERON Having once this juice,   180

I'll watch Titania when she is asleep

And drop the liquor of it in her eyes.

The next thing then she, waking, looks upon,

(Be it on lion, bear, or wolf, or bull,

On meddling monkey, or on busy ape)   185

She shall pursue it with the soul of love.

And ere I take this charm from off her sight,

(As I can take it with another herb),

At a fair virgin, a ruler in the west,

And sent his love-arrow quickly from his bow,

Enough to pierce a hundred thousand hearts.

But I saw that young Cupid's fiery shaft

Was quenched in the chaste beams of the watery moon,   165

And the royal lady passed on

In maidenly meditation, quite free.

Yet I took note of where that bolt of Cupid's fell.

It fell upon a little western flower;

Before, milk white, now purple with love's wound—   170

And maidens call it "love-in-idleness."

Bring me that flower, the herb I showed you once.

The juice of it, laid on sleeping eyelids,

Will make man or woman madly love

The next live creature that is seen.   175

Bring me this herb, and be back here again

Before the whale can swim three miles.

PUCK   I'll make a circle around the earth

    In forty minutes.

Exit PUCK

OBERON   When I have this juice,   180

    I'll watch Titania when she is asleep,

    And drop the liquor of it in her eyes.

    The next thing she sees when she awakes—

    Be it a lion, bear, or wolf, or bull,

    A meddling monkey, or a busy ape—   185

    She will pursue it with the soul of love.

    And before I'll take the spell from her sight,

    As I can do with another herb,

I'll make her render up her page to me.

But who comes here? I am invisible,   190

And I will overhear their conference.

         Enter DEMETRIUS, HELENA *following him*

DEMETRIUS I love thee not, therefore pursue me not.

Where is Lysander and fair Hermia?

The one I'll slay, the other slayeth me.

Thou told'st me they were stol'n unto this wood,   195

And here am I, and wood within this wood,

Because I cannot meet my Hermia.

Hence, get thee gone, and follow me no more.

HELENA You draw me, you hard-hearted adamant;

But yet you draw not iron, for my heart   200

Is true as steel. Leave you your power to draw,

And I shall have no power to follow you.

DEMETRIUS Do I entice you? Do I speak you fair?

Or rather do I not in plainest truth

Tell you I do not nor I cannot love you?   205

HELENA And even for that do I love you the more.

I am your spaniel; and, Demetrius,

The more you beat me, I will fawn on you.

Use me but as your spaniel: Spurn me, strike me,

Neglect me, lose me; only give me leave,   210

Unworthy as I am, to follow you.

What worser place can I beg in your love—

And yet a place of high respect with me—

Than to be used as you use your dog?

DEMETRIUS Tempt not too much the hatred of my spirit,   215

I'll make her give that page boy to me.

But who's coming? I am invisible,   190

And I'll overhear their conversation.

            Enter DEMETRIUS, *followed by* HELENA

DEMETRIUS I don't love you, so don't pursue me.

Where are Lysander and fair Hermia?

The one I'll slay, the other slays me.

You said they had stolen into this wood;   195

And here am I, gone mad within this wood,

Because I can't find my Hermia.

So go away and don't follow me anymore.

HELENA You draw me to you, hard-hearted magnet.

But it is not iron that you draw, for my heart   200

Is true as steel. Give up your power to attract

And I won't be drawn to follow you.

DEMETRIUS Do I lead you on? Do I flatter you?

Or rather don't I in plainest truth

Tell you that I do not and cannot love you?   205

HELENA And just for saying that, I love you even more.

I am your spaniel and, Demetrius,

The more you beat me, the more I fawn on you.

Treat me like your spaniel: Reject me, strike me,

Neglect me, lose me, but allow me,   210

Unworthy though I am, to follow you.

What lower place in your life could I have—

And yet a place I'd proudly have—

Than to be treated as you treat your dog?

DEMETRIUS Don't tempt my hatred too far,   215

For I am sick when I do look on thee.

HELENA And I am sick when I look not on you.

DEMETRIUS You do impeach your modesty too much

    To leave the city and commit yourself

    Into the hands of one that loves you not,   220

    To trust the opportunity of night

    And the ill counsel of a desert place

    With the rich worth of your virginity.

HELENA Your virtue is my privilege. For that

    It is not night when I do see your face,   225

    Therefore I think I am not in the night.

    Nor doth this wood lack worlds of company,

    For you, in my respect, are all the world.

    Then how can it be said I am alone

    When all the world is here to look on me?   230

DEMETRIUS I'll run from thee and hide me in the brakes,

    And leave thee to the mercy of wild beasts.

HELENA The wildest hath not such a heart as you.

    Run when you will. The story shall be changed:

    Apollo flies, and Daphne holds the chase;   235

    The dove pursues the griffin; the mild hind

    Makes speed to catch the tiger—bootless speed,

    When cowardice pursues and valor flies.

DEMETRIUS I will not stay thy questions. Let me go!

    Or, if thou follow me, do not believe   240

    But I shall do thee mischief in the wood.

HELENA Ay, in the temple, in the town, the field,

Because I'm sick of the sight of you.

HELENA And I'm sick when I can't see you.

DEMETRIUS You're risking your reputation too much

 To leave the city and place yourself

 In the hands of a man who doesn't love you,   220

 To trust the opportunity of night

 And the dangers of a deserted place

 With your valuable virginity.

HELENA Your virtue is my guarantee of safety.

 When I see you it isn't night,   225

 So I don't think of this as night—

 Nor is this wood at all deserted,

 For in my mind you are the whole world.

 So how can it be said I am alone

 When all the world is here with me?   230

DEMETRIUS I'll run from you and hide myself in the bushes

 And leave you at the mercy of wild beasts.

HELENA The wildest can't be as cruel as you.

 Run if you want, the old myth shall be changed:

 Apollo flies, and Daphne chases him,   235

 The dove pursues the lion, the mild deer

 Makes speed to catch the tiger. Pointless speed,

 When cowardice pursues and valor flies.

DEMETRIUS I won't stay to argue—let me go;

 Or, if you follow me, you can be sure   240

 That I'll do you mischief in the wood.

HELENA Yes, in the temple, in the town, the field,

You do me mischief. Fie, Demetrius!

Your wrongs do set a scandal on my sex.

We cannot fight for love, as men may do; 245

We should be wooed and were not made to woo.

Exit DEMETRIUS

I'll follow thee and make a heaven of hell,

To die upon the hand I love so well.

[*She follows after*]

OBERON Fare thee well, nymph. Ere he do leave this grove,

Thou shalt fly him, and he shall seek thy love. 250

Enter PUCK

Hast thou the flower there? Welcome, wanderer.

PUCK Ay, there it is.

OBERON I pray thee, give it me.

I know a bank where the wild thyme blows,

Where oxlips and the nodding violet grows, 255

Quite overcanopied with luscious woodbine,

With sweet muskroses, and with eglantine.

There sleeps Titania sometime of the night,

Lulled in these flowers with dances and delight.

And there the snake throws her enamelled skin, 260

Weed wide enough to wrap a fairy in.

And with the juice of this I'll streak her eyes,

And make her full of hateful fantasies.

Take thou some of it, and seek through this grove.

A sweet Athenian lady is in love 265

With a disdainful youth. Anoint his eyes—

But do it when the next thing he espies

May be the lady. Thou shalt know the man

You do me mischief. Shame, Demetrius!
Your behavior offends all women.
We cannot fight for love as men can do;   245
We should be wooed and not have to woo.

Exit DEMETRIUS

I'll follow you and make a heaven of hell,
Even to die by the hand I love so well.

Exit HELENA

OBERON Farewell, maiden. Before he leaves this grove
You'll fly from him, and he shall seek your love.   250

Enter PUCK

Have you the flower there? Welcome, wanderer.
PUCK Yes, there it is.
OBERON Then please give it to me.
I know a bank where the wild thyme blows,
Where oxlips and the nodding violet grows,   255
Quite overcanopied with luscious woodbine,
With sweet muskroses and with eglantine.
Sometimes Titania sleeps there at night,
Lulled in these flowers by dances and delight.
And there the snake sheds her enamelled skin,   260
Wide enough to wrap a fairy in.
And with the juice of this, I'll streak her eyes,
And make her full of frightening fantasies.
You take some of it and search through this grove.
A sweet Athenian lady is in love   265
With a scornful youth; anoint his eyes—
But do it so that the next thing he spies
Will be the lady. You will know the man

By the Athenian garments he hath on.

Effect it with some care, that he may prove   270

More fond on her than she upon her love.

And look thou meet me ere the first cock crow.

PUCK Fear not, my lord! Your servant shall do so.

Exit

Scene 2 [*Another part of the wood*]

Enter TITANIA *and her train*

TITANIA Come, now a roundel and a fairy song;

Then, for the third part of a minute, hence—

Some to kill cankers in the muskrose buds,

Some war with reremice for their leathern wings

To make my small elves coats, and some keep back   5

The clamorous owl that nightly hoots and wonders

At our quaint spirits. Sing me now asleep;

Then to your offices, and let me rest.

[FAIRIES sing as TITANIA *lies down within a bower*]

FIRST FAIRY You spotted snakes, with double tongue,

Thorny hedgehogs, be not seen.   10

Newts and blindworms do no wrong,

Come not near our Fairy Queen.

CHORUS Philomel, with melody

Sing in our sweet lullaby,

Lulla, lulla, lullaby; lulla, lulla, lullaby.   15

By the Athenian clothing he's wearing.

Do this carefully, so he takes a whim   270

To love her more than she loves him.

Then be sure to meet me before first cock crow,

PUCK   Don't worry, my lord, your servant shall do so.

Exit all

Scene 2   [*Another part of the forest*]

Enter TITANIA *and her attendants*

TITANIA   Come, now a ring dance and a fairy song;

Then for the third of a minute, go away—

Some to kill the worms in the musk rose buds,

Some to fight with bats for their leathern wings

To make my small elves coats, and some keep away   5

The noisy owl that nightly hoots and puzzles

At our pretty dance. Sing me to sleep now,

Then go about your duties and let me rest

[FAIRIES sing as TITANIA *lies down within a bower*]

FIRST FAIRY   You spotted snakes, with double tongue,

Thorny hedgehogs, be not seen;   10

Newts and blindworms do no wrong,

Come not near our Fairy Queen.

CHORUS   Philomel, with melody,

Sing in our sweet lullaby,

Lulla, lulla, lullaby; lulla, lulla, lullaby.   15

   Never harm,

   Nor spell, nor charm,

  Come our lovely lady nigh.

  So good night, with lullaby.

FIRST FAIRY Weaving spiders come not here;   20

  Hence you long-legged spinners, hence!

  Beetles black approach not near;

  Worm nor snail do no offense.

CHORUS Philomel, with melody,

   Sing in our sweet lullaby,   25

  Lulla, lulla, lullaby; lulla, lulla, lullaby.

   Never harm,

   Nor spell, nor charm,

  Come our lovely lady nigh.

  So goodnight with lullaby.   30

[TITANIA *sleeps*]

SECOND FAIRY Hence, away! Now all is well.

  One aloof stand sentinel.

           Exeunt FAIRIES

 Enter OBERON *who squeezes the flower juice on* TITANIA'S *eyelids*

OBERON What thou seest when thou dost wake,

  Do it for thy true love take.

  Love and languish for his sake.   35

  Be it ounce, or cat, or bear,

  Pard, or boar with bristled hair,

  In thy eye that shall appear

          Never harm,

          Nor spell, nor charm,

        Do from our lovely lady fly.

        So good night, with lullaby.

FIRST FAIRY Weaving spiders come not here; 20

          Away, long-legged spinners, hence;

          Beetles black approach not near;

          Worm or snail do no offense.

CHORUS   Philomel, with melody,

          Sing in our sweet lullaby— 25

        Lulla, lulla, lullaby; lulla, lulla, lullaby.

          Never harm,

          Nor spell nor charm;

        Do from our lovely lady fly.

        So good night, with a lullaby. 30

[TITANIA *sleeps*]

SECOND FAIRY Hence, away, now all is well.

        One stand apart as sentinel.

                   Exit FAIRIES

   Enter OBERON *who squeezes flower juice on* TITANIA'S *eyelids*

OBERON What you first see when you awake,

        Do it for your true love take;

        Love and suffer for his sake. 35

        Be it lynx, or cat, or bear,

        Leopard, boar with bristled hair,

        In your eyes what does appear

When thou wak'st, it is thy dear.

Wake when some vile thing is near. 40

Exit

Enter LYSANDER *and* HERMIA

LYSANDER Fair love, you faint with wand'ring in the wood.

   And, to speak troth, I have forgot our way.

   We'll rest us, Hermia, if you think it good,

   And tarry for the comfort of the day.

HERMIA Be it so, Lysander; find you out a bed, 45

   For I upon this bank will rest my head.

LYSANDER One turf shall serve as pillow for us both;

   One heart, one bed, two bosoms, and one troth.

HERMIA Nay, good Lysander. For my sake, my dear,

   Lie further off yet; do not lie so near. 50

LYSANDER O take the sense, sweet, of my innocence!

   Love takes the meaning in love's conference.

   I mean that my heart unto yours is knit,

   So that but one heart we can make of it;

   Two bosoms interchained with an oath, 55

   So then two bosoms and a single troth.

   Then by your side no bed-room me deny,

   For lying so, Hermia, I do not lie.

HERMIA. Lysander riddles very prettily.

   Now much beshrew my manners and my pride, 60

   If Hermia meant to say Lysander lied.

   But, gentle friend, for love and courtesy.

   Lie further off, in human modesty.

   Such separation, as may well be said,

When you waken, it's your dear.

Wake when some vile thing is near! 40

Exit OBERON

Enter LYSANDER *leading* HERMIA

LYSANDER Fair love, you're weak from wandering in the wood;

And, to tell the truth, I've lost our way.

Let's rest here, Hermia, if you think it good,

And wait until the break of day.

HERMIA Yes, let's, Lysander. Find a place for your bed; 45

And upon this bank I'll rest my head.

LYSANDER One patch of grass can serve as pillow for us now—

One heart, one bed, two bosoms, and one vow.

HERMIA No, good Lysander, for my sake, my dear,

Lie further off, do not lie so near. 50

LYSANDER Oh, take the true sense, sweet, of my remark!

Love should see its meaning even in the dark.

I mean that my heart to yours is so joined,

It's not yours and mine but ours combined.

Two bosoms intertwined from now, 55

So then two bosoms and a single vow.

Then by your side no bed-room me deny,

For lying so, Hermia, I do not lie.

HERMIA Lysander explains very prettily.

Now shame on my manners and my pride, 60

If Hermia meant to say Lysander lied.

But, gentle friend, for love and courtesy,

Lie further off, in courteous modesty.

Such separation it can be said

Becomes a virtuous bachelor and a maid,   60

So far be distant; and good night, sweet friend,

Thy love ne'er alter till thy sweet life end.

LYSANDER Amen, amen, to that fair prayer, say I,

And then end life when I end loyalty!

Here is my bed. Sleep give thee all his rest.   65

HERMIA With half that wish the wisher's eyes be pressed.

[*They sleep*]

PUCK *appears*

PUCK Through the forest have I gone,

But Athenian found I none

On whose eyes I might approve

This flower's force in stirring love.   75

Night and silence—Who is here?

Weeds of Athens he doth wear.

This is he, my master said,

Despised the Athenian maid;

And here the maiden, sleeping sound,   80

On the dank and dirty ground.

Pretty soul, she durst not lie

Near this lack-love, this kill-courtesy.

Churl, upon thy eyes I throw

All the power this charm doth owe.   85

When thou wak'st, let love forbid

Sleep his seat on thy eyelid.

He squeezes the flower juice on LYSANDER'S *eyelids*

So awake when I am gone;

For I must now to Oberon.

Exit PUCK

Suits a virtuous bachelor and a maid, 65

So sleep over there, and good night, sweet friend,

May your love never alter till your sweet life end.

LYSANDER Amen, amen, to that good prayer, say I—

May my life end when I end loyalty!

Here is my bed. Sleep give you all his rest. 70

HERMIA With half that wish, may your eyes be pressed.

[*They sleep*]

Enter PUCK

PUCK Through the forest have I gone,

But Athenian found I none

On whose eyes I could prove

This flowers's power to stir love. 75

Night and silence! Who is here?

Clothes of Athens he does wear.

This is he, my master said,

Who rejected the Athenian maid.

And here's the maiden, sleeping sound, 80

On the damp and dirty ground.

Pretty soul, she dares not lie

Near this lack-love, this kill-courtesy.

Boor, upon your eyes I throw

All the power this charm does owe. 85

When you awaken, love will keep

Your eyes from closing in sweet sleep.

He squeezes flower juice on LYSANDER'S *eyelids*

So awaken when I am gone;

I must go to Oberon.

Exit PUCK

Enter DEMETRIUS *and* HELENA, *running*

HELENA   Stay, though thou kill me, sweet Demetrius!   90

DEMETRIUS   I charge thee, hence, and do not haunt me thus.

HELENA   O, wilt thou darkling leave me? Do not so.

DEMETRIUS   Stay, on thy peril! I alone will go.

Exit DEMETRIUS

HELENA   O, I am out of breath in this fond chase!

    The more my prayer, the lesser is my grace.   95

    Happy is Hermia, wheresoe'er she lies,

    For she hath blessed and attractive eyes.

    How came her eyes so bright? Not with salt tears—

    If so, my eyes are oft'ner washed than hers.

    No, no, I am as ugly as a bear,   100

    For beasts that meet me run away for fear.

    Therefore no marvel though Demetrius

    Do, as a monster, fly my presence thus.

    What wicked and dissembling glass of mine

    Made me compare with Hermia's sphery eyne?   105

    But who is here? Lysander on the ground!

    Dead—or asleep? I see no blood, no wound.

    Lysander, if you live, good sir, awake.

LYSANDER [*Leaps up*]   And run through fire I will, for thy sweet sake.

    Transparent Helena! Nature shows art,   110

    That through thy bosom makes me see thy heart.

    Where is Demetrius? O, how fit a word

    Is that vile name to perish on my sword!

Enter DEMETRIUS, *followed by* HELENA

HELENA Stop, even if you kill me, sweet Demetrius.   90

DEMETRIUS Clear off and do not haunt me thus!

HELENA Oh, would you leave me in darkness? Don't do so.

DEMETRIUS Stay, take your chances. Alone I'll go.

Exit DEMETRIUS

HELENA Oh, I'm out of breath from chasing you!

The more I pray, the less comes true.   95

Hermia is happy, wherever she lies,

For she has blessed and attractive eyes.

What makes her eyes so bright? Not salt tears—

If so, my eyes are oftener washed than hers.

No, no, I am ugly as a bear,   100

Beasts that meet me run away in fear.

Therefore it's no wonder Demetrius

Flies me as if from something monstrous.

How did my wicked mirror tell lies,

Make me compare mine with Hermia's star-bright eyes?   105

But who's this? Lysander! On the ground!

Dead or asleep? I see no blood, no wound.

Lysander, if you live, good sir, awake.

LYSANDER [*Leaping up*] And run through fire for your sweet sake.

Beautiful Helena! Nature shows her art,   110

So through your manner, I can see your heart.

Where is Demetrius? Oh, how fit a word

Is that vile name to perish on my sword!

HELENA Do not say so, Lysander, say not so.

    What though he love your Hermia? Lord, what though?   115

    Yet Hermia still loves you. Then be content.

LYSANDER Content with Hermia? No! I do repent

    The tedious minutes I with her have spent.

    Not Hermia, but Helena I love—

    Who will not change a raven for a dove?   120

    The will of man is by his reason swayed,

    And reason says you are the worthier maid.

    Things growing are not ripe until their season;

    So I, being young, till now was not ripe to reason.

    And touching now the point of human skill,   125

    Reason becomes the marshal to my will

    And leads me to your eyes; where I o'erlook

    Love's stories, written in Love's richest book.

HELENA Wherefore was I to this keen mockery born?

    When at your hands did I deserve this scorn?   130

    Is't not enough, is't not enough, young man,

    That I did never, no, nor never can,

    Deserve a sweet look from Demetrius' eye,

    But you must flout my insufficiency?

    Good troth, you do me wrong, good sooth, you do,   135

    In such disdainful manner me to woo.

    But fare you well. Perforce I must confess

    I thought you lord of more true gentleness.

    O, that a lady, of one man refused,

    Should of another therefore be abused!   140

                         Exit HELENA

LYSANDER She sees not Hermia. Hermia, sleep thou there,

HELENA Don't say that, Lysander, don't say that.

    Even though he loves your Hermia, what of it?   115

    Hermia still loves you, so be content.

LYSANDER Content with Hermia? No! I do repent

    The tedious minutes I with her have spent.

    Not Hermia, but Helena I love—

    Who wouldn't change a raven for a dove?   120

    The will of man is by his reason swayed;

    And reason says you are the worthier maid.

    Growing things are not ripe until their season;

    So I, being young, had not ripened yet to reason—

    But now that I have a more mature skill,   125

    Reason becomes the guide to my will

    And leads me to your eyes, where I can look

    At Love's stories, written in Love's finest book.

HELENA Why am I the victim of your mockery?

    Why have you become so scornful of me?   130

    Isn't it bad enough, young man,

    That I never have and never can

    Win a sweet look from Demetrius' eye,

    But you must make fun of my inadequacy?

    My word, you do me wrong, truly you do,   135

    In such a scornful manner to pretend to woo,

    But goodbye now, I'm forced to confess

    I thought you a man of more true gentleness.

    Oh, that a lady by one man refused,

    Should by another man be so abused!   140

                           Exit HELENA

LYSANDER She didn't see Hermia. Hermia, sleep right there,

And never mayst thou come Lysander near.
For, as a surfeit of the sweetest things
The deepest loathing to the stomach brings,
Or as the heresies that men do leave   145
Are hated most of those they did deceive,
So thou, my surfeit and my heresy,
Of all be hated, but the most of me!
And all my powers, address your love and might
To honor Helen, and to be her knight.   150

Exit LYSANDER

HERMIA [*Awaking*] Help me, Lysander, help me. Do thy best
To pluck this crawling serpent from my breast.
Ay me, for pity! What a dream was here!
Lysander, look how I do quake with fear.
Methought a serpent eat my heart away,   155
And you sat smiling at his cruel prey.
Lysander! What, removed? Lysander! Lord!
What, out of hearing? Gone? No sound, no word?
Alack, where are you? Speak, an if you hear.
Speak, of all loves! I swoon almost with fear.   160
No? Then I will perceive you are not nigh.
Either death or you I'll find immediately.

Exit

And never to Lysander come near.

For, as excess of the sweetest things

The deepest loathing to the stomach brings,

Or as the convert leaves in haste   145

All the heresies he once embraced,

So you are excess and heresy,

To be hated most by me!

And all my powers, their love and might,

Will honor Helena and be her knight.   150

Exit LYSANDER

HERMIA [*Awaking*] Help me, Lysander, help me; do your best

To pluck this crawling serpent from my breast,

Oh, me, for pity sake! What dream was here!

Lysander, look how I do shake with fear.

I thought a serpent ate up my heart,   155

And you sat smiling at his cruel sport.

Lysander! Have you gone? Lysander! Lord!

What, out of hearing? Gone? No sound, no word?

Alas, where are you? Speak, if you can hear;

Speak, if you love me! I almost faint with fear.   160

No? Then I gather you are not nearby.

Either death or you I'll find immediately.

Exits

Act Three

Scene 1 [*Another part of the woods*]

    Enter QUINCE, SNUG, BOTTOM, FLUTE, SNOUT, *and* STARVELING

BOTTOM Are we all met?

QUINCE Pat, pat. And here's a marvelous convenient place for
    our rehearsal. This green plot shall be our stage, this
    hawthorn-brake our tiring-house—and we will do it
    in action as we will do it before the Duke.　　　　　　5

BOTTOM Peter Quince!

QUINCE What say'st thou, bully Bottom?

BOTTOM There are things in this comedy of Pyramus and
    Thisbe that will never please. First, Pyramus must draw
    a sword to kill himself, which the ladies cannot abide.　　10
    How answer you that?

SNOUT By'r lakin, a parlous fear.

STARVELING I believe we must leave the killing out,
    when all is done

BOTTOM Not a whit. I have a device to make all well.　　15
    Write me a prologue, and let the prologue seem to say
    we will do no harm with our swords, and that Pyramus
    is not killed indeed; and, for the more better assurance,
    tell them that I, Pyramus, am not Pyramus, but Bottom
    the weaver. This will put them out of fear.　　　　　20

QUINCE Well, we will have such a prologue, and it
    shall be written in eight and six.

BOTTOM No, make it two more; let it be written in
    eight and eight.

Act Three

Scene 1   [*Another part of the woods*]

  Enter QUINCE, SNUG, BOTTOM, FLUTE, SNOUT *and* STARVELING

BOTTOM   Are we all here?

QUINCE   On the dot, and here's a wonderfully convenient
  place for our rehearsal. This green plot shall be our
  stage, this hawthorn bush our dressing room—and we
  will perform it just as we will before the Duke.   5

BOTTOM   Peter Quince!

QUINCE   What is it, good Bottom?

BOTTOM   There are things in this comedy of Pyramus
  and Thisbe that will never work. First, Pyramus must
  draw a sword to kill himself, which the ladies will not stand for.   10
  What about that?

SNOUT   By Our Lady, that is a serious matter.

STARVELING   I believe we must leave all the killing out,
  when all is said and done.

BOTTOM   Not at all. I have an idea to make all well.   15
  Write me a prologue and let the prologue say that we will
  do no harm with our swords, and that Pyramus is not killed
  at all. And, to reassure them, tell them that I, Pyramus,
  am not Pyramus at all, but Bottom the weaver. This will
  calm their fears.   20

QUINCE   Well, we will have such a prologue, and it shall
  be written in lines of eight, then six syllables.

BOTTOM   No, add two syllables and let it be written in
  eight and eight.

SNOUT Will not the ladies be afeard of the lion?   25

STARVELING I fear it, I promise you.

BOTTOM Masters, you ought to consider with yourself:
    to bring in (God shield us!) a lion among ladies is
    a most dreadful thing. For there is not a more fearful
    wildfowl than your lion living; and we ought to look to't.   30

SNOUT Therefore, another prologue must tell he is not
    a lion.

BOTTOM Nay, you must name his name, and half his
    face must be seen through the lion's neck, and he himself
    must speak through, saying thus, or to the same defect: 35
    "Ladies," or "Fair ladies, I would wish you," or "I would
    request you," or "I would entreat you, not to fear, not to
    tremble! My life for yours. If you think I come hither
    as a lion, it were pity of my life. No! I am no such
    thing. I am a man as other men are." And there indeed   40
    let him name his name, and tell them plainly he is Snug
    the joiner.

QUINCE Well, it shall be so. But there is two hard things:
    that is, to bring the moonlight into a chamber, for you
    know, Pyramus and Thisbe meet by moonlight.   45

SNOUT Doth the moon shine that night we play our
    play?

BOTTOM A calendar, a calendar! Look in the almanac.
    Find out moonshine, find out moonshine.

QUINCE *takes out a book*

SNOUT   Won't the ladies be afraid of the lion?   25

STARVELING   I fear so, I can tell you.

BOTTOM   Fellows, you ought to reconsider—

    to bring in (God help us) a lion among ladies is

    a dreadful thing, for there is not a more fearful wild

    thing living than your lion, and we ought to reconsider.   30

SNOUT   Therefore, another prologue must tell that he is not

    a lion.

BOTTOM   No, you must also name his name, and half his

    face must be seen through the lion's neck, and he himself

    must speak through it and say something to the defect,   35

    "Ladies," or "Fair ladies—I would wish you," or "I would

    request you," or "I would entreat you, not to fear, not to

    tremble. I am no threat. If you think I'm really a lion,

    I'd be ashamed. No, I am no such thing. I am a man

    like other men." And then indeed have him give   40

    his name, and tell them plainly he is Snug the

    joiner.

QUINCE   Well, it shall be so, but here are two problems:

    First, how do we bring moonlight into a room?

    For you know Pyramus and Thisbe meet by moonlight   45

SNOUT   Does the moon shine on the night we give our

    play?

BOTTOM   A calendar, a calendar! Look in the almanac.

    See if there's a moon, see if there's a moon.

QUINCE *takes out a book*

QUINCE Yes, it doth shine that night. 50

BOTTOM Why, then may you leave a casement of the
Great Chamber window, where we play, open, and the
moon may shine in at the casement.

QUINCE Ay, or else one must come in with a bush of
thorns and a lantern, and say he comes to disfigure or to 55
present the person of Moonshine. Then, there is another
thing: We must have a wall in the Great Chamber; for
Pyramus and Thisbe, says the story, did talk through
the chink of a wall.

SNOUT You can never bring in a wall. What say you, 60
Bottom?

BOTTOM Some man or other must present Wall. And let
him have some plaster, or some loam, or some roughcast
about him, to signify wall; and let him hold his fingers
thus [*he stretches out his fingers*] and through that 65
cranny shall Pyramus and Thisbe whisper.

QUINCE If that may be, then all is well [*takes out a
book and opens it*] Come, sit down, every mother's son,
and rehearse your parts. Pyramus, you begin. When
you have spoken your speech, enter into that brake; 70
and so every one according to his cue.

Enter PUCK

PUCK What hempen homespuns have we swagg'ring here,
So near the cradle of the Fairy Queen?
What, a play toward? I'll be an auditor,
An actor too perhaps, if I see cause. 75

QUINCE Speak, Pyramus. Thisbe, stand forth.

QUINCE Yes, it does shine that night.   50

BOTTOM Why then you can leave one of the windows of
the Great Chamber, where we perform, open, and the
moon will shine in at the window.

QUINCE Right, or else someone must come in with a bush of
thorns and a lantern and say he comes to disfigure or to   55
present the person of Moonshine. Then there is another
thing: We must have a wall in the Great Chamber; for
Pyramus and Thisbe, says the story, talked through a
chink in the wall.

SNOUT You can never bring in a wall. What do you say,   60
Bottom?

BOTTOM Some man or other must present Wall, and let
him have some plaster, or some earth, or some clay
on him to suggest a wall, and let him hold his
fingers thus [*making a horizontal V*] and through   65
that chink Pyramus and Thisbe can whisper.

QUINCE If we do that, it will be fine [*takes out a
book and opens it*]. Come, sit down, everyone,
and rehearse your parts. Pyramus, you begin. When
you have spoken your lines, go behind that bush,   70
and so everyone listen for your cue.

                 Enter PUCK *unseen*

PUCK What rustic homespuns have we carrying on here,
So near the bower of the Fairy Queen?
What, a play in rehearsal? I'll be audience;
An actor too perhaps, if I see a reason.   75

QUINCE Speak, Pyramus. Thisbe, stand by.

BOTTOM   Thisbe, the flowers of odious savors sweet—

QUINCE [*prompts*]   "Odorous, odorous!"

BOTTOM   —odorous savors sweet.

>So hath thy breath, my dearest Thisbe dear.   80

>But hark, a voice! Stay thou but here awhile,

>And by and by I will to thee appear.

>>>>*Exits into the brake*

PUCK [*aside*]   A stranger Pyramus than e'er played here!

>>>>[*He follows* BOTTOM]

FLUTE   Must I speak now?

QUINCE   Ay, marry, must you. For you must understand   85
he goes but to see a noise that he heard, and is to
come again.

FLUTE   Most radiant Pyramus, most lily-white of hue,

>Of color like the red rose on triumphant briar,

>Most brisky juvenal, and eke most lovely Jew,   90

>As true as truest horse that yet would never tire,

>I'll meet thee, Pyramus, at Ninny's tomb.

QUINCE   "Ninus' tomb," man! Why, you must not speak
that yet! That you answer to Pyramus. You speak all
your part at once, cues and all. Pyramus, enter. Your   95
cue is past. It is, "never tire."

FLUTE   O!

>As true as truest horse, that yet would never tire.

Enter from the brake BOTTOM *with an ass's head;* PUCK *following*

BOTTOM   If I were fair, Thisbe, I were only thine.

QUINCE   O monstrous! O strange! We are haunted.   100

BOTTOM Thisbe, the flowers have odious sweet smells—

QUINCE Not "odious," "odorous!"

BOTTOM Odorous sweet smells,

So has your breath, my dearest Thisbe dear.   80

But listen, a voice! Wait here awhile,

And by and by I will to you appear.

Exit BOTTOM *behind the bush*

PUCK [*aside*] That's the strangest Pyramus I ever saw!

[*He follows* BOTTOM]

FLUTE Must I speak now?

QUINCE Yes, yes, you must. For you must understand   85

he's only going to see about a noise he heard and then

will come back again.

FLUTE Most radiant Pyramus, most lily white of hue,

Of color like the red rose on triumphant briar,

Most frisky youth, and also most lovely Jew,   90

As true as truest horse that never would tire,

I'll meet you, Pyramus, at Ninny's tomb.

QUINCE "Ninus' tomb," man! But you must not say that line

yet! You answer that to Pyramus. You're saying all

your lines at once, cues and all. Pyramus, enter. Your   95

cue is past. It is "never tire."

FLUTE Oh!

As true as truest horse that yet would never tire.

Enter BOTTOM *wearing ass's head, followed by* PUCK

BOTTOM If I were fair, Thisbe, I'd be only yours.

QUINCE Oh, monstrous! Oh, strange! We are haunted.   100

Pray, masters! Fly, masters! Help!

Exit all but BOTTOM *and* PUCK

PUCK I'll follow you. I'll lead you about a round,

    Through bog, through bush, through brake, through briar.

    Sometime a horse I'll be, sometime a hound,

    A hog, a headless bear, sometime a fire,   105

    And neigh, and bark, and grunt, and roar, and burn,

    Like horse, hound, hog, bear, fire, at every turn.

Exit PUCK

BOTTOM Why do they run away? This is a knavery of them

    to make me afeared.

Enter SNOUT

SNOUT [*peering from behind a bush*] O Bottom, thou art changed!   110

    What do I see on thee?

BOTTOM What do you see? You see an ass-head of your own,

    do you?

Exit SNOUT

Enter QUINCE

QUINCE Bless thee Bottom, bless thee! thou art translated.

Exits

BOTTOM I see their knavery. This is to make an ass of me,   115

    to fright me if they could. But I will not stir from this place,

    do what they can. I will walk up and down here, and

    will sing that they shall hear I am not afraid. [*sings*]

        The ousel cock, so black of hue

        With orange-tawny bill,   120

        The throstle with his note so true,

        The wren with little quill—

Please, men! Fly everyone! Help!

                              Exit all but BOTTOM *and* PUCK

PUCK   I'll follow you; I'll in a circle lead you round,

Through bog, through bush, through brush, through briar.

Sometimes I'll be a horse, sometimes a hound,

A hog, a headless bear, sometimes a fire,   105

And neigh, and bark, and grunt, and roar, and burn,

Like horse, hound, hog, bear, fire, at every turn.

                              Exit PUCK

BOTTOM   Why do they run away? This is a trick of theirs

to frighten me.

                    Enter SNOUT

SNOUT   [*peering from behind a bush*] Bottom, you are changed! What   110

do I see on your head?

BOTTOM   What do you see? You see an ass-head of your own,

do you?

                              Exit SNOUT

                    Enter QUINCE

QUINCE   Bless you, Bottom, bless you. You are transformed.

                              Exit QUINCE

BOTTOM   I see their trickery. This is to make an ass of me,   115

to frighten me, if they could, but I won't leave this place,

whatever they do. I'll walk up and down here, and

I'll sing so they can hear I'm not afraid. [*sings*]

The blackbird that's so dark of hue

With orange tawny bill   120

The thrush with his note so true,

The wren with little quill—

TITANIA [*comes from the bower*] What angel wakes
    me from my flow'ry bed?

BOTTOM [*sings*] The finch, the sparrow, and the lark,   125
    The plain-song cuckoo gray,

    Whose note full many a man doth mark,

    And dares not answer,"nay"—

for, indeed, who would set his wit to so foolish a bird? Who

would give a bird the lie, though he cry "cuckoo" never so?   130

TITANIA I pray thee, gentle mortal, sing again!

Mine ear is much enamored of thy note,

So is mine eye enthralled to thy shape,

And thy fair virtue's force—perforce—doth move me,

On the first view, to say, to swear, I love thee.   135

BOTTOM Methinks, mistress, you should have little reason

for that. And yet, to say the truth, reason and love keep

little company together nowadays. The more the pity,

that some honest neighbors will not make them friends.

Nay, I can gleek upon occasion.   140

TITANIA Thou art as wise as thou art beautiful.

BOTTOM Not so, neither; but if I had wit enough to get

out of this wood, I have enough to serve mine own turn.

TITANIA Out of this wood do not desire to go!

Thou shalt remain here, whether thou wilt or no.   145

I am a spirit of no common rate,

The summer still doth tend upon my state,

And I do love thee. Therefore go with me.

I'll give thee fairies to attend on thee,

TITANIA [*awaking*] What angel wakes me
       from my flowery bed?

BOTTOM [*sings*] The finch, the sparrow, and the lark,   125
       The plain-song cuckoo gray;
       Whose note full many a man does mark,
       And dares not answer, "nay"—
for, indeed, who would match his wits with so foolish a bird?
Who would call it a liar, no matter how much it cried "cuckoo"?   130

TITANIA I beg you, gentle mortal, sing again!
       My ear is delighted by your melody,
       And my eye is spellbound by your figure,
       And the power of your excellence compels me
       On first sight to say, to swear, I love what I see.   135

BOTTOM I think, lady, you should have little reason
       for that. And yet, to tell the truth, reason and love
       hardly go together these days. And it's a pity
       that someone cannot make them go together.
       Well, I can make a clever joke on occasion.   140

TITANIA You are as wise as you are beautiful.

BOTTOM Not really, but if I had wit enough to get
       out of this wood, that's really all I'd need.

TITANIA Out of this wood do not desire to go!
       You'll remain here whether you want to or no.   145
       I am a spirit of no ordinary rank;
       Summer on my presence does bank.
       And I do love you, so come along, do—
       I'll provide fairies to wait on you.

And they shall fetch thee jewels from the deep,   150
And sing while thou on pressed flowers dost sleep.
And I will purge thy mortal grossness so
That thou shalt like an airy spirit go.
[*she calls*] Peaseblossom, Cobweb, Moth, and Mustardseed!

        Enter fairies as she utters each name

PEASEBLOSSOM Ready!   155

COBWEB And I!

MOTH And I!

MUSTARDSEED And I!

ALL [*bowing*] Where shall we go?

TITANIA Be kind and courteous to this gentleman.   160
    Hop in his walks and gambol in his eyes;
    Feed him with apricocks and dewberries,
    With purple grapes, green figs, and mulberries;
    The honey-bags steal from the humble-bees,
    And for night-tapers crop their waxen thighs   165
    And light them at the fiery glowworm's eyes,
    To have my love to bed and to arise;
    And pluck the wings from painted butterflies
    To fan the moonbeams from his sleeping eyes.
    Nod to him, elves, and do him courtesies.   170

PEASEBLOSSOM Hail! mortal!

COBWEB Hail!

MOTH Hail!

MUSTARDSEED Hail!

BOTTOM I cry your worship's mercy, heartily. I beseech 175

They shall bring you gems from the sea so deep,   150
And sing while on pressed flowers you sleep.
I'll wipe away all that makes you mortal, so
That you can like an airy spirit go.
[*she calls*] Peaseblossom, Cobweb, Moth, and Mustardseed!

Enter FAIRIES

PEASEBLOSSOM Ready!   155

COBWEB And I!

MOTH And I!

MUSTARDSEED And I!

ALL [*bowing*] Where shall we go?

TITANIA Be kind and courteous to this gentleman.   160
Frolic around him in full view of his eyes,
Feed him with apricots and blackberries,
With purple grapes, green figs, and mulberries;
Steal the honeybags from the bumble-bees,
And for candles cut off their waxen thighs,   165
And light them from the glowworm's eyes,
To light my love to bed and to arise;
And pluck the wings from painted butterflies,
To fan the moonbeams from his sleeping eyes.
Bow to him, elves, and pay him courtesies.   170

PEASEBLOSSOM Hail mortal!

COBWEB Hail!

MOTH Hail!

MUSTARDSEED Hail!

BOTTOM And I say hail to you, too. I beg to know   175 your worship's name.

COBWEB [*bows*] Cobweb.

BOTTOM I shall desire you of more acquaintance, good
    Master Cobweb. If I cut my finger, I shall make bold
    with you. Your name, honest gentleman?   180

PEASEBLOSSOM [*bows*] Peaseblossom.

BOTTOM I pray you, commend me to Mistress Squash,
    your mother, and to Master Peascod, your father.
    Good Master Peaseblossom, I shall desire you of more
    acquaintance too. Your name, I beseech you, sir?   185

MUSTARDSEED [*bows*] Mustardseed.

BOTTOM Good Master Mustardseed, I know your
    patience well. That same cowardly, giant-like oxbeef
    hath devoured many a gentleman of your house. I
    promise you, your kindred hath made my eyes water   190
    ere now. I desire you of more acquaintance, good
    Master Mustardseed.

TITANIA Come, wait upon him. Lead him to my bower.
    The moon, methinks, looks with a wat'ry eye,
    And when she weeps, weeps every little flower,   195
    Lamenting some enforced chastity.
    Tie up my love's tongue. Bring him silently.

Exit

your name, sir.

COBWEB [*bows*] Cobweb.

BOTTOM I'll want to know you better, good
    Master Cobweb. If I cut my finger, I'll use you
    as a bandage. Your name, honest gentleman?   180

PEASEBLOSSOM [*bows*] Peaseblossom.

BOTTOM Please give my regards to Mistress Squash,
    your mother, and to Master Peapod, your father.
    Good Master Peaseblossom, I'll want to know you
    better, too. Your name, I ask, sir?   185

MUSTARDSEED [*bows*] Mustardseed.

BOTTOM Good Master Mustardseed, I know how patient
    you are. All those cowardly giant sides of beef
    have used up many gentlemen of your family. I
    tell you, your relatives have made my eyes water   190
    many a time. I wish to know you better,
    good Master Mustardseed.

TITANIA Come, wait upon him; lead him to my bower.
    I think the moon looks with misty eye,
    And when she weeps so does every little flower   195
    About some offense against chastity.

[BOTTOM *brays like a donkey*]

    Tie up my love's tongue, bring him silently.

                  All exit

Scene 2 [*Another part of the wood*]

Enter OBERON

OBERON I wonder if Titania be awaked.

Then what it was next came in her eye,

Which she must dote on in extremity.

Enter PUCK

Here comes my messenger. How now, mad spirit?

What night-rule now about this haunted grove?   5

PUCK My mistress with a monster is in love.

Near to her close and consecrated bower,

While she was in her dull and sleeping hour,

A crew of patches, rude mechanicals

That work for bread upon Athenian stalls,   10

Were met together to rehearse a play

Intended for great Theseus' nuptial day.

The shallowest thickskin of that barren sort,

Who Pyramus presented in their sport

Forsook his scene and ent'red in a brake.   15

When I did him at his advantage take,

An ass's noll I fixed on his head.

Anon his Thisbe must be answered,

And forth my mimic comes. When they him spy,

As wild geese that the creeping fowler eye,   20

Or russet-pated choughs, many in sort,

Rising and cawing at the gun's report,

Sever themselves and madly sweep the sky,

So, at his sight, away his fellows fly,

And, at our stamp, here o'er and o'er one falls.   25

He "murder" cries, and help from Athens calls.

Their sense thus weak, lost with their fears thus strong,

Scene 2 [*Another part of the wood*]

Enter OBERON

OBERON   I wonder if Titania has awakened;

And what it was she first did spy

That now she loves excessively.

Enter PUCK

Here comes my messenger. What happened, wild sprite?

What's going on in this haunted grove tonight?   5

PUCK   Titania in a monster takes delight.

Near to her secret and holy bower,

While she was drowsy in her sleeping hour,

A bunch of workman, crude mechanics all

That sell their work in Athenian stalls,   10

Were gathered to rehearse a play

Intended for great Theseus' wedding day.

The dumbest of that empty-headed sort,

Who played Pyramus in their sport,

Left the stage to hide behind a limb;   15

So I quickly took advantage of him,

And put an ass's head upon his head.

He went to answer what Thisbe said,

And took his place. When they him spy,

They ran as geese from hunter's eye,   20

Or like red-headed crows in fear of being caught,

Rise cawing and flapping at the sound of gunshot

They scatter and madly sweep the sky,

So, at sight of him, his friends did fly.

And when I stamped my foot, they tumbled away   25

One crying "murder," another prayed.

With their senses so weak and their fears so strong,

Made senseless things begin to do them wrong.

For briars and thorns at their apparel snatch,

Some sleeve, some hats; from yielders all things catch. 30

I led them on in this distracted fear,

And left sweet Pyramus translated there.

When in that moment (so it came to pass)

Titania waked and straightway loved an ass.

OBERON This falls out better than I could devise! 35

But hast thou yet latched the Athenian's eyes

With the love juice, as I did bid thee do?

PUCK I took him sleeping—that is finished, too—

And the Athenian woman by his side,

That, when he waked, of force she must be eyed. 40

Enter DEMETRIUS *and* HERMIA

OBERON Stand close. This is the same Athenian.

PUCK This is the woman; but not this the man.

DEMETRIUS O, why rebuke you him that loves you so?

Lay breath so bitter on your bitter foe.

HERMIA Now I but chide; but I should use thee worse, 45

For thou, I fear, hast given me cause to curse.

If thou hast slain Lysander in sleep,

Being o'er shoes in blood, plunge in the deep,

And kill me too.

The sun was not so true unto the day 50

As he to me. Would he have stolen away

From sleeping Hermia? I'll believe as soon

This whole earth may be bored, and that the moon

May through the center creep and so displease

Inanimate things seemed to do them wrong.

For briars and thorns at their clothing snatch;

In their fright they let hats, sleeves, all things, catch.   30

I led them away in their distracted fear,

And left sweet Pyramus transformed here.

Just at that moment (so it came to pass)

Titania waked and straightway loved an ass.

OBERON Why this turned out better than I could ask.   35

But did you find the Athenian, your other task,

And drop the love juice, as I bid you do?

PUCK I saw him sleeping—that is finished too.

And the Athenian woman by his side,

When he awakens, she will be spied.   40

Enter DEMETRIUS *and* HERMIA

OBERON Stand close. This is the same Athenian.

PUCK This is the woman, but this is not the man.

DEMETRIUS Oh, why do you scold me when I love you so?

Save your bitter comments for your bitter foe.

HERMIA Now I only scold, but I'll say worse   45

If I find you've given me the cause to curse.

If you've slain Lysander in his sleep,

Are ankle-deep in blood, then plunge the knife

And kill me too.

The sun was not as faithful to the day   50

As Lysander was to me. Would he have crept away

From sleeping Hermia? I'd believe as soon

That the earth had a hole and that the moon

Could creep through the center and decide

Her brother's noontide with the Antipodes. 55

It cannot be but thou hast murdered him.

So should a murderer look, so dead, so grim.

DEMETRIUS So should the murdered look, and so should I,

Pierced through the heart with your stern cruelty.

Yet you, the murderer, look as bright, as clear, 60

As yonder Venus in her glimmering sphere.

HERMIA What's this to my Lysander? Where is he?

Ah, good Demetrius, wilt thou give him me?

DEMETRIUS I had rather give his carcass to my hounds.

HERMIA Out, dog! Out, cur! Thou driv'st me past the bounds 65

Of maiden's patience. Hast thou slain him then?

Henceforth be never numbered among men!

O, once tell true! tell true, even for my sake!

Durst thou have looked upon him, being awake?

And hast thou killed him sleeping? O brave touch! 70

Could not a worm, an adder, do so much?

An adder did it; for with doubler tongue

Than thine (thou serpent) never adder stung.

DEMETRIUS You spend your passion on a misprised mood.

I am not guilty of Lysander's blood; 75

Nor is he dead for aught that I can tell.

HERMIA I pray thee, tell me then that he is well.

DEMETRIUS An if I could, what should I get therefore?

HERMIA A privilege never to see me more;

To disrupt the sun's path on the other side.   55

It must be that you have murdered him.

You look like a killer—so deadly, so grim.

DEMETRIUS So does a victim look, and so should I,

Pierced through the heart with your stern cruelty.

Yet you, the murderer, look as bright and clear,   60

As the yonder star of Venus does appear.

HERMIA How does this concern Lysander? Where is he?

Oh, please Demetrius, give him to me.

DEMETRIUS I'd rather give his carcass to my hounds.

HERMIA Out, dog! Out, cur! You drive me past the bounds   65

Of maidenly patience. Have you slain him then?

From now on, don't consider yourself human.

Oh, tell me the truth! the truth! Just for my sake!

Did you see him when you were awake?

And then kill him as he slept? Oh, brave touch!   70

Couldn't a snake or an adder do as much?

A snake did do it; for even an adder's tongue

Was not so forked as yours when you stung.

DEMETRIUS You spend your anger in a wasteful flood.

I'm not guilty of spilling Lysander's blood;   75

Nor is he dead, for all I can tell.

HERMIA I beg you then, tell me he's well.

DEMETRIUS And if I do, what would I get then?

HERMIA The privilege of never seeing me again.

And from thy hated presence part I so.   80

See me no more whether he be dead or no.

Exit HERMIA

DEMETRIUS There is no following her in this fierce vein;

Here therefore for a while I will remain.

So sorrow's heaviness doth heavier grow

For debt that bankrout sleep doth sorrow owe;   85

Which now in some slight measure it will pay,

If for his tender here I make some stay.

[*Lies down and sleeps*]

OBERON What hast thou done? Thou hast mistaken quite

And laid the love juice on some true-love's sight.

Of thy misprision must perforce ensue   90

Some true-love turned, and not a false turned true.

PUCK Then fate o'errules, that, one man holding troth,

A million fail, confounding oath on oath.

OBERON About the wood go swifter than the wind,

And Helena of Athens look thou find.   95

All fancy-sick is she, and pale of cheer

With sighs of love, that cost the fresh blood dear.

By some illusion see thou bring her here.

I'll charm his eyes against she do appear.

PUCK I go, I go! Look how I go!   100

Swifter than an arrow from the Tartar's bow.

Exit PUCK

OBERON [*applying love juice to Demetrius' eyes*]

Flower of this purple dye,

Hit with Cupid's archery,

And from your hated presence I'll now go.   80
See me no more, whether he be dead or no.

Exit HERMIA

DEMETRIUS No use following her; she's in an angry mood.
Therefore, I'll stay and rest awhile in this wood.
The weight of sorrow even heavier seems
Since I've had no sleep to dream sweet dreams.   85
So now I'll take time to make that right,
By sleeping here awhile this night.

[*Lies down and sleeps*]

OBERON What have you done? You have mistaken quite
And laid the love juice on some true love's sight.
Because of your mistake, it now seems as though   90
True love has turned false, but false is still so.

PUCK Fate overruled your plan. One man may be true,
But millions are not and break oaths as they woo.

OBERON Go about the wood swifter than the wind,
And Helena of Athens be sure to find.   95
She's all love sick with a face so pale
Her sighs for love will make her heart fail.
By some illusion make sure to bring her here.
I'll charm his eyes when she does appear.

PUCK I go! I go! Look how I go!   100
Swifter than an arrow from a soldier's bow.

Exit PUCK

OBERON [*applying love juice to Demetrius's eyes*]
        Flower of this purple dye,
        Hit with Cupid's archery,

Sink in apple of his eye!
When his love he doth espy,   105
Let her shine as gloriously
As the Venus of the sky.
When thou wak'st, if she be by,
Beg of her for remedy.

Enter PUCK

PUCK   Captain of our fairy band,   110
Helena is here at hand,
And the youth, mistook by me,
Pleading for a lover's fee.
Shall we their fond pageant see?
Lord, what fools these mortals be!   115

OBERON   Stand aside; the noise they make
Will cause Demetrius to awake.

PUCK   Then will two at once woo one.
That must needs be sport alone.
And those things do best please me   120
That befall prepost'rously.

Enter LYSANDER *and* HELENA

LYSANDER   Why should you think that I should woo in scorn?
Scorn and derision never come in tears.
Look, when I vow, I weep; and vows so born,
In their nativity all truth appears.   125
How can these things in me seem scorn to you,
Bearing the badge of faith to prove them true?

HELENA   You do advance your cunning more and more.

Pierce the pupil of his eye!

When his love he can spy, 105

Let her shine as gloriously

As Venus in the sky.

When you waken, if she is near,

Beg her to be your lover dear.

Enter PUCK

PUCK   Captain of our fairy band, 110

Helena is here at hand,

And the youth mistook by me,

Pleading for a lover's fee.

Shall we their silly scene now see?

Lord, what fools these mortals be! 115

OBERON   Stand aside, the noise they make

Will cause Demetrius to awake

PUCK   Then two at once will woo one.

That will be the best joke done;

And those things do please me best 120

That turn out a preposterous jest.

Enter LYSANDER *and* HELENA

LYSANDER   Why should you think that I woo in scorn?

If I derided and scorned, would I shed tears?

Look, when I vow, I weep, and vows so born,

Prove by their birth that truth appears. 125

How can these things seem like scorn to you,

When they are like a badge to prove my love is true?

HELENA   You display your cunning more and more.

When truth kills truth. O devilish holy fray!
These vows are Hermia's. Will you give her o'er?　　　　130
Weigh oath with oath, and you will nothing weigh.
Your vows to her and me, put in two scales,
Will even weigh, and both light as tales.

LYSANDER　I had no judgement when to her I swore.

HELENA　Nor none, in my mind, now you give her o'er.　　135

LYSANDER　Demetrius loves her, and he loves not you.

DEMETRIUS [*waking*]　O Helen, goddess, nymph, perfect,
　　　　divine!
To what, my love, shall I compare thine eyne?
Crystal is muddy. O, how ripe in show　　　　140
Thy lips, those kissing cherries, tempting grow!
That pure congealed white, high Taurus' snow,
Fanned with the eastern wind, turns to crow
When thou hold'st up thy hand. O, let me kiss
This princess of pure white, this seal of bliss!　　　　145

HELENA　O spite! O hell! I see you all are bent
To set against me for your merriment.
If you were civil and knew courtesy,
You would not do me thus much injury.
Can you not hate me, as I know you do,　　　　150
But you must join in souls to mock me too?
If you were men, as men you are in show,
You would not use a gentle lady so,
To vow, and swear, and superpraise my parts,
When I am sure you hate me with your hearts.　　　　155

If this vow's true, the other one is betrayed.

These vows are meant for Hermia. Have you deserted her?   130

If you measure your oaths, there's nothing weighed.

Your vows to her and me, put in two scales,

Will weigh evenly, both as light as tales.

LYSANDER I had no sense when I swore to her.

HELENA Nor none now, to my mind, to throw her over!   135

LYSANDER Demetrius loves her; he doesn't love you.

DEMETRIUS [*waking*] Helena! Goddess, nymph, perfection

      in you lies!

To what, my love, can I compare your eyes?

Crystal is muddy. Oh, how ripe, I see,   140

Are your lips, like cherries, tempting me!

That frozen, pure white mountain snow,

Cooled by eastern wind, turns black, you know

When I compare it with your hand. Let me kiss

This queenly whiteness, and seal my bliss!   145

HELENA Oh spite! Oh hell! I see you all consent

  To gang up against me for your merriment.

If you were polite and knew courtesy,

You would not do me so much injury.

You hate me, yes I know you do,   150

But must you conspire to mock me too?

If you were men, as men you are in show,

You would not treat a gentle lady so;

To vow and swear and overpraise my parts,

When I'm sure you hate me with all your hearts.   155

You both are rivals and love Hermia.

And now both rivals to mock Helena.

A trim exploit, a manly enterprise,

To conjure tears up in a poor maid's eyes

With your derision! None of noble sort　　　　　160

Would so offend a virgin and extort

A poor soul's patience, all to make your sport.

LYSANDER　You are unkind, Demetrius, be not so!

For you love Hermia, this you know I know;

And here, with all good will, with all my heart,　　165

In Hermia's love I yield you up my part.

And yours of Helena to me bequeath,

Whom I do love, and will do till to my death.

HELENA　Never did mockers waste more idle breath.

DEMETRIUS　Lysander, keep thy Hermia, I will none.　　170

If e'er I loved her, all that love is gone.

My heart to her but as guestwise sojourned,

And now to Helen is it home returned,

There to remain.

LYSANDER　Helen, it is not so.　　　　　　　175

DEMETRIUS　Disparage not the faith thou dost not know,

Lest, to thy peril, thou aby it dear.

Look where thy love comes; yonder is thy dear.

Enter HERMIA

HERMIA　Dark night, that from the eye his function takes,

The ear more quick of apprehension makes.　　　180

You both are rivals and love Hermia.

Now you compete to mock Helena.

What a fine thing, a manly enterprise,

To bring the tears to a poor maid's eyes

With your mockery! None of the noble sort   160

Would so offend a virgin and extort

A poor soul's patience, just to have some sport.

LYSANDER   You are unkind, Demetrius. Be not so!

For you love Hermia; this you know we know;

So here, with all good will, with all my heart,   165

Of Hermia's love I yield you up my part.

Now give up claims to Helena, I cry.

I'll worship her till the day I die.

HELENA   Never did mockers so waste a lie.

DEMETRIUS   Lysander, keep your Hermia. I want none;   170

If ever I loved her, that love is gone.

My heart was only loaned to her,

It's home with Helena and will not stir,

But there remains.

LYSANDER   Helena, it's not so.   175

DEMETRIUS   Don't insult the faith you don't know,

Or you might find you buy it at great cost.

But see who comes here, looking lost.

Enter HERMIA

HERMIA   The dark night takes away my sight,

But makes my hearing much more bright.   180

Wherein it doth impair the seeing sense,

It pays the hearing double recompense.

Thou art not by mine eye, Lysander, found;

Mine ear, I thank it, brought me to thy sound.

But why unkindly didst thou leave me so? 185

LYSANDER Why should he stay whom love doth press to go?

HERMIA What love would press Lysander from my side?

LYSANDER Lysander's love, that would not let him bide,

Fair Helena, who more engilds the night

Than all yon fiery oes and eyes of light. 190

Why seek'st thou me? Could not this make thee know,

The hate I bear thee made me leave thee so?

HERMIA You speak not as you think. It cannot be.

HELENA Lo, she is one of this confederacy!

Now I perceive they have conjoined all three 195

To fashion this false sport in spite of me.

Injurious Hermia! Most ungrateful maid!

Have you conspired, have you with these contrived,

To bait me with this foul derision?

Is all the counsel that we two have shared, 200

The sisters' vows, the hours that we have spent

When we have chid the hasty-footed time

For parting us—O, is all forgot?

All schooldays' friendship, childhood innocence?

We, Hermia, like two artificial gods, 205

Have with our needles created both one flower,

Although it might impair the seeing sense
It pays the hearing double recompense.
Lysander, you were not by my eyes found,
It was my ear, I thank it, that brought me to your sound.
But why unkindly did you leave me so?   185
LYSANDER   Why would I stay when love pressed me to go?
HERMIA   What love would draw Lysander from where he lay?
LYSANDER   Lysander's love, that would not let him stay,
    Fair Helena, who more decorates the night
    Than all the stars, those eyes of light.   190
    Why did you follow me? Why didn't you know
    The hate I bear you made me leave you so?
HERMIA   You don't really mean what you say. It cannot be.
HELENA   Look, she is part of this conspiracy!
    Now I understand they have conspired all three   195
    To think up these lies and mock at me.
    Insulting Hermia! Most traitorous maid!
    Have you conspired, have you connived with these
    To torment me with this cruel ridicule?
    Are all the secrets that we two have shared,   200
    The vows to be sisters, the hours spent
    When we scolded time for hurrying by
    And parting us—Oh, is that forgotten?
    All schooldays' friendships, childhood innocence?
    We, Hermia, like two craftsmen,   205
    With our needles have created a flower together,

Both on one sampler, sitting on one cushion,
Both warbling of one song, both in one key;
As if our hands, our sides, voices, and minds
Had been incorporate. So we grew together, 210
Like to a double cherry, seeming parted,
But yet an union in partition—
Two lovely berries molded on one stem;
So, with two seeming bodies, but one heart;
Two of the first, like coats in heraldry, 215
Due but to one, and crowned with one crest.
And will you rent our ancient love asunder,
To join with men in scorning your poor friend?
It is not friendly, 'tis not maidenly!
Our sex, as well as I, may chide you for it, 220
Though I alone do feel the injury.

HERMIA I am amazed at your passionate words.
I scorn you not. It seems you scorn me.

HELENA Have you not set Lysander, as in scorn,
To follow me and praise my eyes and face? 225
And made your other love, Demetrius—
Who even but now did spurn me with his foot—
To call me goddess, nymph, divine, and rare,
Precious, celestial? Wherefore speaks he this
To her he hates? And wherefore doth Lysander 230
Deny your love, so rich within his soul,
And tender me, forsooth, affection,
But by your setting on, by your consent?
What though I be not so in grace as you,

Working on one tapestry, sitting on one cushion,

Singing one song, both together in one key;

As if our hands, our sides, voices, and minds

Had been combined in one. So we grew together,   210

Like a double cherry, seeming separate,

But yet united even in division—

Two lovely berries growing on one stem;

So, with two bodies, but one heart,

Like a coat of arms divided into parts   215

But all crowned with one crest.

Will you tear apart our long friendship,

To join with men in scorning your poor friend?

It is not friendly, it's not maidenly!

All women, not just I, will scold you for it,   220

Though only I feel the injury.

HERMIA   I am amazed at your passionate words.

    I don't scorn you, you seem to scorn me.

HELENA   Haven't you urged Lysander to mockingly

    Follow me and praise my eyes and face?   225

    And made your other love, Demetrius

    Who only a short while ago kicked me away—

    Call me goddess, nymph, divine, and rare,

    Precious, celestial? Why would he say this

    To one he hates? And why does Lysander   230

    Deny he loves you—you, his soulmate—

    And pretend, for goodness sake, he loves me,

    If not at your urging, by your consent?

    Even though I'm not as popular as you

So hung upon with love, so fortunate, 235
But miserable most, to love unloved?
This you should pity rather than despise.

HERMIA I understand not what you mean by this.

HELENA Ay, do! Persever, counterfeit sad looks,
Make mouths upon me when I turn my back, 240
Wink each at other, hold the sweet jest up.
This sport, well carried, shall be chronicled.
If you have any pity, grace, or manners,
You would not make me such an argument.
But fare ye well. 'Tis partly my own fault, 245
Which death or absence soon shall remedy.

LYSANDER Stay, gentle Helena; hear my excuse,
My love, my life, my soul, fair Helena!

HELENA O excellent!

HERMIA [to LYSANDER] Sweet, do not scorn her so. 250

DEMETRIUS If she cannot entreat, I can compel.

LYSANDER Thou canst compel no more than she entreat.
Thy threats have no more strength than her weak prayers.
Helen, I love thee. By my life, I do!
I swear by that which I will lose for thee 255
To prove him false that says I love thee not.

DEMETRIUS I say I love thee more than he can do.

LYSANDER If thou say so, withdraw and prove it too.

DEMETRIUS Quick, come!

HERMIA [takes hold of LYSANDER] Lysander, whereto tends all this? 260

As covered with caresses, as fortunate;   235

Instead, I'm miserable and unloved by him I love,

Shouldn't you pity rather than despise me?

HERMIA I don't understand what you mean by this.

HELENA Yes, keep it up, fake sad looks,

Make faces at me behind my back,   240

Wink at each other, keep up the joke.

This sport, if carried off, will become a legend.

If you have any pity, grace, or manners,

You would not make me such a figure of fun.

But farewell to you. It's partly my own fault,   245

Which death or absence will soon mend.

LYSANDER Stay, gentle Helena; hear my excuse,

My love, my life, my soul, fair Helena!

HELENA Oh, excellent!

HERMIA [to LYSANDER] Sweetheart, don't scorn her so.   250

DEMETRIUS And if she cannot make you stop, I can.

LYSANDER You cannot any more than she can

Your threats have no more strength than her weak prayers.

Helena, I love you, I swear I do!

I swear by my life, which I'll give for you,   255

To prove anyone false who says I don't love you.

DEMETRIUS I say I love you more than he can do.

LYSANDER If you say so, step over here and prove it too.

DEMETRIUS Quick, come on!

HERMIA [takes hold of LYSANDER] Lysander, what does all this mean? 260

LYSANDER Away, you Ethiope!

DEMETRIUS [*to* HERMIA] No, no. He'll

    Seem to break loose. [*to* LYSANDER] Take on as you
        would follow,

    But come not. You are a tame man, go!   265

LYSANDER [*to* HERMIA] Hang off, thou cat, thou burr! Vile thing, let loose,

    Or I will shake thee from me like a serpent!

HERMIA Why are you grown so rude? What change is this,

    Sweet love?

LYSANDER Thy love? Out, tawny Tartar, out!   270

    Out loathed med'cine! O hated potion, hence!

HERMIA Do you not jest?

HELENA Yes, sooth! And so do you.

LYSANDER Demetrius, I will keep my word with thee.

DEMETRIUS I would I had your bond; for I perceive   275

    A weak bond holds you. I'll not trust your word.

LYSANDER What, should I hurt her, strike her, kill her dead?

    Although I hate her, I'll not harm her so.

HERMIA What, can you do me greater harm than hate?

    Hate me? Wherefore? O me! What news, my love?   280

    Am not I Hermia? Are not you Lysander?

    I am as fair now as I was erewhile.

    Since night you loved me; yet since night you left me.

    Why then, you left me—O, the gods forbid!—

LYSANDER Get away, you Ethiop!

DEMETRIUS [*to* HERMIA] No, no. He'll

    Pretend to break away from her and

        follow me,

    [*to* LYSANDER] But then you won't. Come on, coward!   265

LYSANDER [*to* HERMIA] Let me go, you cat, you burr! Vile thing, let go,

    Or I'll shake you from me like a snake!

HERMIA Why do you act so rude? What change is this,

    Sweet love?

LYSANDER Your love? Out, dark-skinned savage, out!   270

    Out, dreaded medicine! Oh, hated potion, away!

HERMIA Are you joking?

HELENA Yes, truly, and so are you.

LYSANDER Demetrius, I meant what I said.

DEMETRIUS I wish I had your bond, for I think   275

    A weak bond holds you there. I don't trust your word.

LYSANDER What can I do, hurt her, strike her, kill her dead?

    Although I hate her, I'll not harm her.

HERMIA How can you do me greater harm than hate?

    Hate me? Why? Oh, my! What news is this, my love?   280

    Aren't I Hermia? Aren't you Lysander?

    I am as beautiful now as I ever was.

    Just this night you loved me, but since then you left me.

    Does that mean—Oh, the gods forbid!—

In earnest, shall I say?   285
LYSANDER Ay, by my life!

And never did desire to see thee more.

Therefore be out of hope, of question, doubt.

Be certain, nothing truer, 'tis no jest

That I do hate thee, and love Helena.   290

[HERMIA *releases him*]

HERMIA O me! [*to* HELENA] You juggler! You canker blossom!

You thief of love! What, have you come by night

And stol'n my love's heart from him?

HELENA Fine, i'faith!

Have you no modesty, no maiden shame,   295

No touch of bashfulness? What, will you tear

Impatient answers from my gentle tongue?

Fie, fie! you counterfeit, you puppet you!

HERMIA "Puppet"? Why, so! Ay, that way goes the game.

Now I perceive that she hath made compare   300

Between our statures; she hath urged her height,

And with her personage, her tall personage,

Her height, forsooth, she hath prevailed with him.

And are you grown so high in his esteem

Because I am so dwarfish and so low?   305

How low am I, thou painted maypole? Speak!

How low am I? I am not yet so low

But that my nails can reach unto thine eyes.

HELENA I pray you, though you mock me, gentlemen,

You've left me for good? 285

LYSANDER Yes, I swear it!

And I hope never to see you again.

Therefore give up hope, don't question or doubt it;

Be certain, there's nothing truer, it's no joke

That I do hate you and love Helena. 290

[HERMIA *releases him*]

HERMIA Oh my! [*to* HELENA] You trickster! You worm in the rose!

You thief of love! What, have you come by night

And stolen my love's heart from him?

HELENA Well, by my faith!

Have you no modesty, no maidenly shame, 295

No touch of bashfulness? What, will you tear

Harsh answers from my gentle tongue?

Shame, shame, you cheat, you puppet, you!

HERMIA "Puppet"? Why, so! Yes, that's the way it goes.

Now I see that she has made a comparison 300

Between our statures; she has bragged of her height

And with her personage, her tall personage,

Her height, I say, she has won him over.

Are you grown so high in his esteem

Because I am so dwarfish and so low? 305

How low am I, you painted maypole? Speak!

How low am I? I am not quite so low

That my nails cannot reach up to your eyes.

HELENA I beg you gentlemen, though you mock me,

Let her not hurt me. I was never curst;   310

I have no gift at all in shrewishness.

I am a right maid for my cowardice.

Let her not strike me. You perhaps may think,

Because she is something lower than myself,

That I can match her.   315

HERMIA   "Lower"? Hark, again!

HELENA   Good Hermia, do not be so bitter with me.

I evermore did love you, Hermia,

Did ever keep your counsels, never wronged you;

Save that, in love unto Demetrius,   320

I told him of your stealth unto this wood.

He followed you; for love, I followed him;

But he hath chid me hence, and threatened me

To strike me, spurn me, nay, to kill me too.

And now, so you will let me quiet go,   325

To Athens will I bear my folly back

And follow you no further. Let me go.

You see how simple and how fond I am.

HERMIA   Why, get you gone! Who is't that hinders you?

HELENA   A foolish heart, that I leave here behind.   330

HERMIA   What, with Lysander?

HELENA   With Demetrius.

LYSANDER   Be not afraid, she shall not harm thee, Helena.

DEMETRIUS   No, sir, she shall not, though you take her part.

Don't let her hurt me. I was never a shrew; 310
I have no skill at all in scolding;
I'm known for being timid.
Don't let her hit me. Perhaps you may think,
Because she is somewhat lower than myself,
That I'm a match for her. 315

HERMIA "Lower"? That again!

HELENA Good Hermia, don't be so bitter toward me.
I always loved you, Hermia,
Always kept your secrets, never wronged you;
Except that, for love of Demetrius, 320
I told him that you stole into this wood.
He followed you; and for love, I followed him;
But he told me to leave and threatened me.
He'd hit me, desert me, even kill me.
And now, if you'll let me go quietly, 325
I'll return with my foolishness to Athens
And follow you no further. Let me go.
You see how simple and silly I am.

HERMIA Why, go on! Who is stopping you?

HELENA Just my foolish heart that I leave here behind. 330

HERMIA What, with Lysander?

HELENA With Demetrius.

LYSANDER Don't be afraid, Helena, she won't hurt you.

DEMETRIUS No, sir, she won't, though Lysander's not much help.

HELENA O, when she is angry, she is keen and shrewd!   335
    She was a vixen when she went to school,
    And though she be but little, she is fierce.
HERMIA "Little" again? Nothing but "low" and "little"?
    Why will you suffer her to flout me thus?
    Let me come to her.   340
LYSANDER Get you gone, you dwarf!
    You minimus of hindering knotgrass made!
    You bead, you acorn—
DEMETRIUS You are too officious
    On her behalf that scorns your services.   345
    Let her alone. Speak not of Helena;
    Take not her part. For if thou dost intend
    Never so little show of love to her,
    Thou shalt aby it.
LYSANDER Now she holds me not.   350
    Now follow, if thou dar'st, to try whose right,
    Of thine or mine, is most in Helena.
DEMETRIUS "Follow"? Nay, I'll go with thee, cheek by jowl.

Exit LYSANDER *and* DEMETRIUS

HERMIA You, mistress, all this coil is long of you.
    Nay, go not back.   355
HELENA I will not trust you, I,
    No longer stay in your curst company.
    Your hands than mine are quicker for a fray;
    My legs are longer though, to run away.

Exit HELENA

HERMIA I am amazed, and know not what to say.   360

Exit HERMIA

106

HELENA Oh, when she is angry, she is sharp and clever! 335

    She was a vixen when she went to school,

    And although she is little, she is fierce.

HERMIA "Little" again? Nothing but "low" and "little"?

    Why do you let her insult me so?

    Let me get at her. 340

LYSANDER Get you gone, you dwarf!

    You midget, nourished on knotgrass!

    You bead, you acorn—

DEMETRIUS You try to take over

    On behalf of one who rejects your services. 345

    Let her alone. Don't mention Helena;

    Don't take her part; for if you try to

    Show any affection to her,

    You'll dearly pay for it.

LYSANDER Now Hermia's not holding me back. 350

    Now follow me if you dare, to see who has the

    Right, you or me, to Helena.

DEMETRIUS Follow you? No, I'll go with you, cheek by jowl.

Exit DEMETRIUS *and* LYSANDER

HERMIA You, miss, all this trouble is because of you.

    No, don't back away. 355

HELENA I will not trust you, I

    Will no longer stay in your rude company.

    Your hands are quicker than mine in a fight;

    My legs are longer though, to run in fright.

Exits

HERMIA I am amazed, and don't know what to say. 360

Exits

OBERON *and* PUCK *come forward*

OBERON This is thy negligence. Still thou mistak'st,

    Or else committ'st thy knaveries wilfully.

PUCK Believe me, king of shadows, I mistook.

    Did not you tell me I should know the man

    By the Athenian garments he had on?   365

    And so far blameless proves my enterprise

    That I have 'nointed an Athenian's eyes;

    And so far am I glad it so did sort,

    As this their jangling I esteem a sport.

OBERON Thou seest these lovers seek a place to fight.   370

    Hie therefore, Robin, overcast the night.

    The stary welkin cover thee anon

    With drooping fog as black as Acheron,

    And lead these testy rivals so astray

    As one come not within another's way.   375

    Like to Lysander sometime frame thy tongue,

    Then stir Demetrius up with bitter wrong.

    And sometime rail thou like Demetrius.

    And from each other look thou lead them thus,

    Till o'er their brows death-counterfeiting sleep   380

    With leaden legs and batty wings doth creep.

    Then crush this herb into Lysander's eye;

[*He gives the flower to* PUCK]

    Whose liquor hath this virtuous property,

    To take from thence all error with his might

    And make his eyeballs roll with wonted sight.   385

OBERON *and* PUCK *come forward*

OBERON This is your carelessness. Mistakes again,

Or else this mischief is done willfully.

PUCK Believe me, king of shadows, I mistook.

Did you not tell me I should know the man

By the Athenian garments he had on?   365

And so blameless is my enterprise

That I have anointed an Athenian's eyes;

And so far I'm glad that it so did run,

As I consider their quarrel fun.

OBERON You see these lovers seek a place to fight.   370

So hurry, Robin, overcast the night.

Cover the starry sky quickly and well

With drooping fog as black as Hell

And lead these angry rivals so astray

That one comes not within another's way.   375

First imitate Lysander with your tongue,

Then stir up Demetrius with bitter wrong;

And sometimes shout just like Demetrius.

And be sure to lead them from each other thus,

Till upon them death-imitating sleep   380

With leaden legs and batlike wings does creep.

Then crush this herb into Lysander's eye;

[*He gives the flower to* PUCK]

Its liquor has the powerful quality,

To take away all error with its might

And make his eyes see with their usual sight.   385

When they next wake, all this derision
Shall seem a dream and fruitless vision.
And back to Athens shall the lovers wend,
With league whose date till death shall never end.
Whiles I in this affair do thee employ, 390
I'll to my queen and beg her Indian boy;
And then I will her charmed eye release
From monster's view, and all things shall be peace.

PUCK   My fairy lord, this must be done with haste,
For night's swift dragons cut the clouds full fast, 395
And yonder shines Aurora's harbinger,
At whose approach ghosts, wand'ring here and there,
Troop home to churchyards. Damned spirits all,
That in crossways and floods have burial,
Already to their wormy beds are gone, 400
For fear lest day should look their shames upon,
They wilfully themselves exile from light,
And must for aye consort with black-browed night.

OBERON   But we are spirits of another sort.
I with the Morning's love have oft made sport, 405
And, like a forester, the groves may tread
Even till the eastern gate, all fiery red,
Opening on Neptune, with fair blessed beams,
Turns into yellow gold his salt green streams.
But notwithstanding, haste! Make no delay. 410
We may effect this business yet ere day.

Exit OBERON

When they awake, these ridiculous events
Will seem but a dream of no significance;
And back to Athens shall the lovers start
To love each other till death does them part.
While I, in this task, do you employ,   390
I'll see my queen and beg her Indian boy;
And then her enchanted eyes I will release
From a monster's spell, and all things shall be peace.
PUCK My fairy lord, this must be done with haste,
For night is passing through the clouds most fast,   395
And over there shines the morning star,
At whose approach, ghosts, wandering here and there,
Troop home to churchyards; all damned spirits,
Buried at crossroads or drowned in floods,
Already to their wormy beds have crept away,   400
For fear their shame will be seen by day,
They willingly exile themselves from light,
And so must ally themselves with night.
OBERON But we are spirits of another sort.
With Aurora's mate I've often made sport,   405
And, like a hunter, I may these groves tread
Even till sunrise, all fiery red,
At the seashore with fair blessed beams
Turns to yellow gold the salt green streams.
But nevertheless, hurry, don't delay;   410
We may finish this work yet before it's day.

Exits

PUCK   Up and down, up and down,

        I will lead them up and down.

        I am feared in field and town.

        Goblin, lead them up and down.   415

   Here comes one.

Enter LYSANDER

LYSANDER Where art thou, proud Demetrius? Speak thou now.

PUCK [*As* DEMETRIUS] Here, villain, drawn and ready. Where art thou?

LYSANDER I will be with thee straight.

PUCK [*As* DEMETRIUS] Follow me, then, to plainer ground.   420

                         Exit LYSANDER

Enter DEMETRIUS

DEMETRIUS Lysander, speak again!

   Thou runaway, thou coward, art thou fled?

   Speak! In some bush? Where dost thou hide thy head?

PUCK [*As* LYSANDER] Thou coward, art thou bragging to the stars,

   Telling the bushes that thou look'st for wars,   425

   And wilt not come? Come, recreant! Come, thou child!

   I'll whip thee with a rod. He is defiled

   That draws a sword on thee.

DEMETRIUS Yea, art thou there?

PUCK [*As* LYSANDER] Follow my voice. We'll try no manhood here.   430

                         They exit

Enter LYSANDER

LYSANDER He goes before me and still dares me on,

   When I come where he calls, then he is gone.

PUCK   Up and down, up and down,

      I will lead them up and down.

      I am feared in field and town.

      Robin, lead them up and down.   415

    Here comes one.

Enter LYSANDER

LYSANDER Where are you, proud Demetrius? Speak up now.

PUCK [*As* DEMETRIUS] Here, villain, drawn and ready. Where are you?

LYSANDER I'll be with you right away.

PUCK [*As* DEMETRIUS] Follow me then to flatter ground.   420

Exit LYSANDER

Enter DEMETRIUS

DEMETRIUS Lysander, speak again!

    You runaway, you coward, have you fled?

    Speak! In some bush? Where do you hide your head?

PUCK [*As* LYSANDER] You coward, are you bragging to the stars,

    Telling the bushes that you look for wars,   425

    And you won't come? Come, coward! Come, you child!

    I'll whip you with a stick. You're much too mild

    For me to draw my sword!

DEMETRIUS Yes, are you there?

PUCK [*As* LYSANDER] Follow my voice. We won't prove manhood here. 430

They exit

Enter LYSANDER

LYSANDER He goes before me and still dares me on.

    When I come where he calls, then he is gone.

The villain is much lighter-heeled than I.
I followed fast, but faster he did fly,
That fallen am I in dark uneven way,   435
And here will rest me. Come, thou gentle day!
For if but once thou show me thy gray light,
I'll find Demetrius and revenge this spite.
[*Lies down and sleeps*]

Enter PUCK *and* DEMETRIUS

PUCK [*As* LYSANDER] Ho, ho, ho! Coward, why com'st thou not?
DEMETRIUS Abide me, if thou dar'st, for well I wot   440
Thou run'st before me, shifting every place,
And dar'st not stand nor look me in the face.
Where art thou now?
PUCK [*As* LYSANDER] Come hither. I am here.
DEMETRIUS Nay, then, thou mock'st me. Thou shalt buy   445
this dear,
If ever I thy face by daylight see.
Now, go thy way. Faintness constraineth me
To measure out my length on this cold bed.
By day's approach look to be visited.   450
[*Lies down and sleeps*]

Enter HELENA

HELENA O weary night, O long and tedious night,
Abate thy hours! Shine comforts from the East,
That I may back to Athens by daylight
From these that my poor company detest.

The villain is swifter-footed than I.

I followed fast, but faster he did fly,

And now I'm on this bumpy ground, 435

So here I'll rest till day comes round.

For once it shows its dim gray light

I'll find Demetrius and revenge this spite.

[*Lies down and sleeps*]

Enter PUCK *and* DEMETRIUS

PUCK [*As* LYSANDER] Ho, ho, ho! Coward, why don't you come, tell.

DEMETRIUS Wait for me, if you dare, for I know well 440

You ran before me, shifting all around,

Not facing up to me or standing your ground.

Where are you now?

PUCK [*As* LYSANDER] Come forward. I am here.

DEMETRIUS No, you're just mocking me. You will pay, 445

that's clear,

If ever your face by daylight I see.

Runaway now. Weariness forces me

To stretch out myself on this cold bed.

When it's daylight look to be visited. 450

[*Lies down and sleeps*]

Enter HELENA

HELENA Oh, weary night. Oh, long and tedious night,

Lessen your hours! Glow, sunshine from the East,

So I can get back to Athens by daylight,

Leaving those who my poor company detest.

And sleep, that sometimes shuts up sorrow's eye,   455
Steal me awhile from mine own company.

[*Lies down and sleeps*]

PUCK   Yet but three? Come one more.
            Two of both kinds makes up four.
            Here she comes, curst and sad.
            Cupid is a knavish lad   460
            Thus to make poor females mad.

                        Enter HERMIA

HERMIA Never so weary, never so in woe.
        Bedabbled with the dew and torn with briars,
        I can no further crawl, no further go.
        My legs can keep no pace with my desires.   465
        Here will I rest me till the break of day.
        Heaven shield Lysander, if they mean a fray!

[*Lies down and sleeps*]

PUCK   On the ground
            Sleep sound.
            I'll apply   470
            To your eye,
            Gentle lover, remedy.

[*Squeezes juice on* LYSANDER's *eyelids*]

            When thou wak'st,
            Thou tak'st
            True delight   475
            In the sight
            Of thy former lady's eye;

And sleep, that sometimes closes a sorrowing eye,   455
Take me away from my own company.
[*Lies down and sleeps*]

PUCK   Yet but three? Come one more.

Two of both kinds make up four.

Here she comes, cross and sad.

Cupid is a naughty lad   460

Thus to make poor females mad.

                Enter HERMIA

HERMIA Never so weary, never so in woe.

Sprinkled with the dew and torn by briars,

I can no further crawl, no further go.

My legs cannot support my desires.   465

I'll rest here till the end of night.

Heaven shield Lysander if they mean to fight.

[*Lies down and sleeps*]

PUCK   On the ground

Sleep sound.

I'll apply   470

To your eye,

Gentle lover, remedy.

[*Squeezes juice on* LYSANDER's *eyelids*]

When you wake,

You will take

True delight   475

In the sight

Of your former lady's eye;

And the country proverb known
That every man should take his own,
In your waking shall be shown. 480
      Jack shall have Jill;
      Naught shall go ill;
The man shall have his mare again, and all shall be well.

Exeunt PUCK

And the country proverb, so well known,
That every man should have his own,
With your waking shall be shown.   480
      Jack shall have Jill;
      Naught shall go ill;
The man shall have his mare again, and all shall be well.

Exits

Act Four

Scene 1 [*The wood.* LYSANDER, DEMETRIUS, HELENA, *and* HERMIA *asleep*]
Enter TITANIA, BOTTOM, *and her train,* OBERON *following*

TITANIA   Come, sit thee down upon this flowery bed,
  While I thy amiable cheeks do coy,
  And stick muskroses in thy sleek smooth head,
  And kiss thy fair large ears, my gentle joy.

BOTTOM   Where's Peaseblossom?   5

PEASEBLOSSOM   Ready.

BOTTOM   Scratch my head, Peaseblossom. Where's
  Monsieur Cobweb?

COBWEB   Ready.

BOTTOM   Monsieur Cobweb, good monsieur, get your   10
  weapons in your hand, and kill me a red-hipped humble-
  bee on the top of a thistle; and good monsieur, bring me
  the honey-bag. Do not fret yourself too much in the
  action, monsieur, and, good monsieur, have a care the
  honey-bag break not. I would be loath to have you over-   15
  flown with a honey-bag, signior. Where's Monsieur
  Mustardseed?

MUSTARDSEED   Ready.

BOTTOM   Give me your neaf, Monsieur Mustardseed. Pray
  you, leave your courtesy, good monsieur.   20

MUSTARDSEED   What's your will?

Act Four

Scene 1 [*The wood.* LYSANDER, DEMETRIUS, HELENA, *and* HERMIA *asleep*]
Enter TITANIA, BOTTOM, *and her attendants*; OBERON *follows*

TITANIA Come, sit here upon this flowery bed,

　　While I your loveable cheeks caress,

　　And stick muskroses on your sleek, smooth head,

　　And kiss your large, fair ears, my joy of gentleness.

BOTTOM Where's Peaseblossom?　　　　　　　　　　　　　　5

PEASEBLOSSOM Ready.

BOTTOM Scratch my head, Peaseblossom. Where's

　　Monsieur Cobweb?

COBWEB Ready.

BOTTOM Monsieur Cobweb, good monsieur, get your　　　10

　　weapons in your hand and kill me a red-hipped bumble-

　　bee on the top of a thistle; and good monsieur, bring me

　　the honey bag. Don't overwork yourself too much in the

　　action, monsieur, and, good monsieur, make sure not

　　to break the honey bag. I would hate to have you　　　15

　　drowned in the honey, signior. Where's Monsieur

　　Mustardseed?

MUSTARDSEED Ready.

BOTTOM Give me your hand, Monsieur Mustardseed. Please

　　never mind the curtsy, good monsieur.　　　　　　　20

MUSTARDSEED What would you like?

BOTTOM Nothing, good monsieur, but to help Cavalery
    Cobweb to scratch. I must to the barber's, monsieur,
    for methinks I am marvelous hairy about the face. And
    I am such a tender ass, if my hair do but tickle me, I must   25
    scratch.

TITANIA What, wilt thou hear some music, my sweet love?

BOTTOM I have a reasonable good ear in music. Let's have
    the tongs and the bones.

TITANIA Or say, sweet love, what thou desirest to eat.   30

BOTTOM Truly, a peck of provender. I could munch your
    good dry oats. Methinks I have a great desire to a bottle of
    hay. Good hay, sweet hay, hath no fellow.

TITANIA I have a venturous fairy that shall seek
    The squirrel's hoard, and fetch thee new nuts.   35

BOTTOM I had rather have a handful or two of dried peas.
    But I pray you, let none of your people stir me. I have an
    exposition of sleep come upon me.

TITANIA Sleep thou, and I will wind thee in my arms.
    Fairies, be gone, and be all ways away.   40

                      Exit FAIRIES

    So doth the woodbine the sweet honeysuckle
    Gently entwist; the female ivy so
    Enrings the barky fingers of the elm.
    O, how I love thee! How I dote on thee!

[*They sleep*]

BOTTOM Nothing, good monsieur, but you to help Cavalier
    Cobweb to scratch. I must get to the barber's, monsieur;
    for I seem to be incredibly hairy about the face. And
    I am such a tender fool, that if my hair tickles me, I must   25
    scratch.

TITANIA Now, would you like some music, my sweet love?

BOTTOM I have a reasonably good ear for music. Let's have
    the tongs and the bones.

TITANIA Or say, sweet love, what you'd like to eat.   30

BOTTOM Truly, a peck of fodder. I could munch some
    good dry oats. I think I would like a bundle of hay.
    Good hay, sweet hay, has no equal.

TITANIA I have an adventurous fairy who will find
    The squirrel's hoard and bring you new nuts.   35

BOTTOM I'd rather have a handful or two of dried peas.
    But, please, don't let anyone awaken me. I have
    an overwhelming desire to sleep.

TITANIA Sleep then, and I will hold you in my arms.
    Fairies, be gone, and guard us on all sides.   40

                         Exit FAIRIES

    So does the woodbine the sweet honeysuckle
    Gently twist round; the female ivy so
    Rings round the barky branches of the elm.
    Oh, how I love you! How excessively I love you!

[*They sleep*]

Enter PUCK

OBERON Welcome, good Robin. Seest thou this sweet sight?   45
　　　Her dotage now I do begin to pity;
　　　For, meeting her of late behind the wood,
　　　Seeking sweet favors for this hateful fool,
　　　I did upbraid her and fall out with her.
　　　For she his hairy temples then had rounded   50
　　　With coronet of fresh and fragrant flowers;
　　　And that same dew which sometime on the buds
　　　Was wont to swell like round and orient peals,
　　　Stood now within the pretty flouriets' eyes,
　　　Like tears that did their own disgrace bewail.   55
　　　When I had at my pleasure taunted her,
　　　And she in mild terms begged my patience,
　　　I then did ask of her her changeling child,
　　　Which straight she gave me, and her fairy sent
　　　To bear him to my bower in Fairyland.   60
　　　And now I have the boy, I will undo
　　　This hateful imperfection of her eyes.
　　　And, gentle Puck, take this transformed scalp
　　　From off the head of this Athenian swain,
　　　That he, awaking when the other do,   65
　　　May all to Athens back again repair,
　　　And think no more of this night's accidents
　　　But as the fierce vexation of a dream.
　　　But first I will release the Fairy Queen.
[*He squeezes the nectar on* TITANIA'S *eyelids*]
　　　　　Be as thou wast wont to be.   70
　　　　　See as thou wast wont to see.

Enter PUCK

OBERON Welcome, good Robin. Do you see this sweet sight?   45

Now I begin to pity her overfondness;

For, meeting her lately behind the wood,

Seeking love tokens for this disgusting fool,

I scolded her and quarreled with her.

For she had encircled his hairy head   50

With coronet of fresh and fragrant flowers;

And that same dew that sometimes on the buds

Lies swollen like round pearls from the Orient,

Stood then in the very heart of the flowers,

Like tears cried for their own disgrace.   55

When I had taken pleasure in taunting her,

And she in mild terms begged my patience,

I then did ask her for her changeling child;

Which she gave me straight away, and sent her fairy

To bring him to my bower in Fairyland.   60

Now that I have the boy, I will undo

The spell I cast upon her eyes.

And, gentle Puck, take this transforming scalp

From off the head of this Athenian lad;

So he, awakening when the others do,   65

May also back to Athens go,

And think no more of this night's incidents

Than the wild puzzlement of a dream.

But first I will release the Fairy Queen.

[*He squeezes nectar on* TITANIA'S *eyelids*]

Be as you used to be.   70

See as you used to see.

Dian's bud o'er Cupid's flower

Hath such force and blessed power.

Now, my Titania! Wake you, my sweet queen.

TITANIA [*Waking*] My Oberon, what visions have I seen!   75

Methought I was enamored of an ass.

OBERON There lies your love.

TITANIA How came these things to pass?

O, how mine eyes do loathe his visage now!

OBERON Silence awhile. Robin, take off this head.   80

Titania, music call; and strike more dead

Than common sleep of all these five the sense.

TITANIA Music, ho, music! Such as charmeth sleep!

PUCK [*Removing the ass-head from* BOTTOM] Now, when thou wak'st,

with thine own fool's eyes peep.   85

OBERON Sound, music! [*music*] Come, my queen, take

hands with me.

And rock the ground whereon these sleepers be.

[*They dance*]

Now thou and I are new in amity,

And will tomorrow midnight solemnly   90

Dance in Duke Theseus' house triumphantly

And bless it to all fair prosperity.

There shall the pairs of faithful lovers be

Wedded, with Theseus, all in jollity.

PUCK   Fairy king, attend and mark.   95

I do hear the morning lark.

OBERON   Then my queen, in silence sad

Diana's bud over Cupid's flower

Has more force and blessed power.

Now, my Titania! Wake you, my sweet queen.

TITANIA [*Waking*] My Oberon, what visions I have seen!　　　75

I thought I was enamored of an ass.

OBERON There lies your love.

TITANIA How came these things to pass?

Oh, my eyes hate to look upon him now!

OBERON Silence awhile. Robin, take off this head.　　　80

Titania, call for music; and strike more dead

Than ordinary sleep the senses of these five.

TITANIA Music, ho, music! Such as charms sleep!

PUCK [*Removing the ass-head from* BOTTOM] Now, when you wake,

Look out of your own silly eyes.　　　85

OBERON Play, music! [*music*] Come, my queen, join

　　　hands with me.

And rock the ground where these five sleepers be.

[*They dance*]

Now you and I again are friendly,

And tomorrow night will solemnly　　　90

Dance in Duke Theseus' house triumphantly

And bless it for all fair prosperity.

There the pairs of faithful lovers shall be

Wedded, with Theseus, all in jollity.

PUCK　　　Fairy King, attend and mark.　　　95

　　　I do hear the morning lark.

OBERON　　　Then my queen, in silence sad

Trip we after night's shade.

We the globe can compass soon,

Swifter than the wand'ring moon. 100

TITANIA   Come, my lord, and in our flight

Tell me how it came this night

That I sleeping here was found

With these mortals on the ground.

Exit TITANIA, OBERON, *and* PUCK

Wind horn. Enter THESEUS, HIPPOLYTA, EGEUS, *and* ATTENDANTS

THESEUS   Go, one of you, find out the forester. 105

For now our observation is performed,

And, since we have the vaward of the day,

My love shall hear the music of my hounds.

Uncouple in the western valley; let them go.

Dispatch, I say, and find the forester. 110

Exit ATTENDANT

We will, fair Queen, up to the mountain's top

And mark the musical confusion

Of hounds and echo in conjunction.

HIPPOLYTA   I was with Hercules and Cadmus once

When in a wood of Crete they bayed the bear 115

With hounds of Sparta. Never did I hear

Such gallant chiding, for, besides the groves,

The skies, the fountains, every region near

Seemed all one mutual cry. I never heard

So musical a discord, such sweet thunder. 120

THESEUS   My hounds are bred out of the Spartan kind,

So flewed, so sanded; and their heads are hung

We leave as night does fade.

Round the globe we'll swifter fly

Than the wandering moon the sky.   100

TITANIA   Come, my lord, and in our flight

Tell me how it came this night

That I, sleeping here was found,

With these mortals on the ground.

Exit TITANIA, OBERON, *and* PUCK

[*Horn sounds.*] *Enter* THESEUS, HIPPOLYTA, EGEUS, *and* ATTENDANTS

THESEUS Go, one of you, and find the forester.   105

For now we have observed the rites of May;

And, since we are still in the vanguard of the day,

My love shall hear the music of my hounds.

Unleash them in the western valley; let them go.

Hurry, I say, and find the forester.   110

Exit ATTENDANT

We'll go, fair Queen, up to the mountain top

And hear the musical confusion

Of hounds and echo in conjunction.

HIPPOLYTA I was with Hercules and Cadmus once,

When in a wood in Crete, they had a bear at bay   115

With hounds of Sparta. Never I heard, I say,

Such gallant barking; for, beside the groves,

The skies, the fountains, every region near

Seemed all one mutual cry. I never did hear

So musical a discord, such sweet thunder.   120

THESEUS My hounds are bred out of the Spartan line,

Mouths folded, fur sand-colored, and heads hung

With ears that sweep away the morning dew;
Crook-kneed, and dewlapped like Thessalian bulls;
Slow in pursuit, but matched in mouth like bells,   125
Each under each. A cry more tuneable
Was never holloed to, nor cheered with horn,
In Crete, in Sparta, nor in Thessaly.
Judge when you hear. But, soft! what nymphs are these?

EGEUS My lord, this is my daughter here asleep,   130
And this Lysander; this Demetrius is,
This Helena, old Nedar's Helena.
I wonder of their being here together.

THESEUS No doubt they rose up early to observe
The rite of May, and hearing our intent,   135
Came here in grace of our solemnity.
But speak, Egeus. Is this not the day
That Hermia should give answer of her choice?

EGEUS It is, my lord.

THESEUS Go, bid the huntsmen wake them with their horns.   140

Exit ATTENDANT

Shout within. Wind horns. The four awake and start up
Good morrow, friends. Saint Valentine is past.
Begin these woodbirds but to couple now?

[*The four kneel*]

LYSANDER Pardon, my lord.

THESEUS I pray you all stand up.

[*They stand up*]

I know you two are rival enemies.   145
How comes this gentle concord in the world,
That hatred is so far from jealousy
To sleep by hate and fear no enmity?

130

With ears that sweep away the morning dew;

Knock-kneed, and jowled like Thessalian bulls;

Slow in pursuit, but matched in barking like bells,   125

Each a different tone; a cry more tuneful

Was never hello'd to, or cheered with horn,

In Crete, in Sparta, nor in Thessaly.

Judge when you hear, but wait! What youths are these?

EGEUS My lord, this is my daughter asleep here;   130

And this, Lysander; this is Demetrius;

This Helena, old Nedar's Helena;

I wonder at their being here together.

THESEUS No doubt they rose up early to observe

The rite of May, and hearing our intent,   135

Came here in honor of our wedding day.

But speak, Egeus. Is this not the day

That Hermia should answer us about her choice?

EGEUS It is, my lord.

THESEUS Go, tell the hunters to wake them with their horns.   140

Exit ATTENDANT

[*Shouting. Horns sound. The four awake and start up*]

Good morning, friends. Valentine's Day is past.

Are these woodbirds only pairing off now?

[*The four kneel*]

LYSANDER Pardon, my lord.

THESEUS Please, all of you, stand up.

[*They stand up*]

I know you two are rival enemies.   145

How comes this gentle peace into the world,

That hatred is so far from jealousy

That you sleep by an enemy and feel no worry?

LYSANDER My lord, I shall reply amazedly,
    Half sleep, half waking. But as yet, I swear,
    I cannot truly say how I came here.   150
    But, as I think (for truly would I speak),
    And now I do bethink me, so it is:
    I came with Hermia hither. Our intent
    Was to be gone from Athens, where we might
    Without the peril of the Athenian law—   155
EGEUS Enough, enough! My lord, you have enough.
    I beg the law, the law, upon his head.
    They would have stol'n away. They would, Demetrius!
    Thereby to have defeated you and me—
    You of your wife, and me of my consent,   160
    Of my consent that she should be your wife.
DEMETRIUS My lord, fair Helen told me of their stealth,
    Of this their purpose hither, to this wood,
    And I in fury hither followed them,
    Fair Helena in fancy following me.   165
    But, my good lord, I wot not by what power
    (But by some power it is) my love to Hermia,
    Melted as the snow, seems to me now
    As the remembrance of an idle gaud
    Which in my childhood I did dote upon,   170
    And all the faith, the virtue of my heart,
    The object and the pleasure of mine eye,
    Is only Helena. To her, my lord,
    Was I betrothed ere I saw Hermia.
    But, like a sickness, did I loathe this food.   175

LYSANDER My lord, I shall reply amazedly,

    Half asleep, half awake. But as yet, I swear,

    I cannot truly say how I came here.   150

    But, I do think (for I wish to speak truthfully),

    And now that I think about it, I'm sure:

    I came here with Hermia. Our intent

    Was to be gone from Athens, where we might

    Without danger of the Athenian law—   155

EGEUS Enough, enough! My lord, you've heard enough!

    I beg the law, the law, upon his head.

    They would have stolen away. They would, Demetrius!

    And thereby defeated you and me—

    You of your wife and me of my consent,   160

    Of my consent that she should be your wife.

DEMETRIUS My lord, fair Helen told me of their flight,

    Of their intent to come to this wood,

    And I followed them here in fury,

    Fair Helena for love following me.   165

    But, my good lord, I know not by what power

    (But by some power it is) my love for Hermia,

    Melted as the snow, seems to me now

    Just the memory of a trivial toy

    That in my childhood I was fond of,   170

    And all the faith, the power of my heart,

    The object and the pleasure of my eyes,

    Is only Helena. To her, my lord,

    I was engaged before I saw Hermia.

    But, like a sickness, I hated this food.   175

But, as in health, come to my natural taste,
Now I do wish it, love it, long for it,
And will for evermore be true to it.

THESEUS Fair lovers, you are fortunately met.
Of this discourse we more will hear anon.   180
Egeus, I will overbear your will,
For in the temple, by and by, with us,
These couples shall eternally be knit.
And, for the morning now is something worn,
Our purposed hunting shall be set aside.   185
Away with us to Athens! Three and three,
We'll hold a feast in great solemnity.
Come, Hippolyta.

Exit THESEUS, HIPPOLYTA, EGEUS, *and* ATTENDANTS

DEMETRIUS These things seem small and undistinguishable,
Like far-off mountains turned into clouds.   190

HERMIA Methinks I see these things with parted eye,
When everything seems double.

HELENA So methinks.
And I have found Demetrius, like a jewel,
Mine own, and not mine own.   195

DEMETRIUS Are you sure
That we are awake? It seems to me
That yet we sleep, we dream. Do not you think
The Duke was here, and bid us follow him?

HERMIA Yea, and my father.   200

But, as in health, come back to normal taste,

Now I do wish it, love it, long for it,

And will forever more be true to it.

THESEUS Fair lovers, it's lucky we've met you.

We'll hear more about this later.   180

Egeus, I will overrule your will;

For in the temple, by and by, with us,

These couples shall eternally be joined.

And, since the morning is almost over,

Our proposed hunting shall be set aside.   185

Come with us to Athens! Three and three,

We'll hold a feast of great festivity.

Come, Hippolyta.

Exit THESEUS, HIPPOLYTA, EGEUS, *and* ATTENDANTS

DEMETRIUS Everything seems vague and hard to make out,

Like far-off mountains turned into clouds.   190

HERMIA I think I see these things with unfocused eyes,

When everything seems double.

HELENA I think so too.

And I have found Demetrius, like a jewel,

My own and not my own.   195

DEMETRIUS Are you sure

That we are awake? It seems to me

That we still sleep and dream. Do you not think

The Duke was here, and told us to follow him?

HERMIA Yes, and my father.   200

HELENA And Hippolyta.

LYSANDER And he did bid us follow to the temple.

DEMETRIUS Why, then, we are awake. Let's follow him,
  And by the way, let us recount our dreams.

Exit

BOTTOM [*Waking up*] When my cue comes, call me, and I will   205
  answer. My next is "Most fair Pyramus." Hey-ho! Peter
  Quince? Flute the bellows-mender? Snout the tinker?
  Starveling? God's my life! Stol'n hence and left me asleep!
  I have had a most rare vision. I have had a dream past
  the wit of man to say what dream it was. Man is but an   210
  ass if he go about to expound this dream. Methought I
  was—there is no man can tell what. Methought I was—and
  methought I had—but man is but a patched fool if he will
  offer to say what methought I had. The eye of man hath
  not heard, the ear of man hath not seen, man's hand is   215
  not able to taste, his tongue to conceive, nor his heart to
  report what my dream was. I will get Peter Quince to
  write a ballad of this dream. It shall be called "Bottom's
  Dream," because it hath no bottom; and I will sing it in
  the latter end of our play before the Duke. Peradventure, to   220
  make it the more gracious, I shall sing it at her death.

Exit

HELENA And Hippolyta.

LYSANDER And he told us to him follow to the temple.

DEMETRIUS Why, then, we are awake. Let's follow him,
     And along the way, let's recount our dreams.

All exit except BOTTOM

BOTTOM [*Waking up*] When my cue comes, call me, and I will   205
     answer. My next line is "Most fair Pyramus." Hey! Peter
     Quince? Flute the bellows-mender? Snout the tinker?
     Starveling? God bless me! Gone away and left me asleep!
     I have had a most rare vision. I have had a dream past
     the wit of man to say what it meant. Man is but an   210
     ass if he thinks he can explain this dream. I thought I
     was —there is no man can tell what. I thought I was—and
     I thought I had—but man is just a clown in jester's colors if he
     will offer to say what I thought I had. The eye of man hasn't
     heard, the ear of man hasn't seen, man's hand is   215
     not able to taste, his tongue to imagine, nor his heart to
     report what my dream was. I will get Peter Quince to
     write a ballad of this dream. It shall be called "Bottom's
     Dream" because it has no bottom; and I will sing it in
     the latter end of our play before the Duke. Maybe, to   220
     make it more pleasing, I shall sing it when Thisbe dies.

Exits

Scene 2 [*Athens. Quince's cottage*]

Enter QUINCE, FLUTE, SNOUT, *and* STARVELING

QUINCE Have you sent to Bottom's house? Is he come
home yet?

STARVELING He cannot be heard of. Out of doubt he is
transported.

FLUTE If he come not, then the play is marred. It goes   5
not forward, doth it?

QUINCE It is not possible. You have not a man in all
Athens able to discharge Pyramus but he.

FLUTE No, he hath simply the best wit of any handicraft
man in Athens.   10

QUINCE Yea, and the best person too, and he is a very
paramour for a sweet voice.

FLUTE You must say "paragon." A "paramour" is (God
bless us) a thing of naught.

Enter SNUG *the joiner*

SNUG Masters, the Duke is coming from the temple, and   15
there is two or three lords and ladies more married. If
our sport had gone forward, we had all been made men.

FLUTE O, sweet bully Bottom! Thus hath he lost six
pence a day during his life. He could not have 'scaped six
pence a day. An the Duke had not given him six pence   20
a day for playing Pyramus, I'll be hanged! He would have
deserved it. Six pence a day in Pyramus, or nothing!

Scene 2 [*Athens. Quince's cottage*]

Enter QUINCE, FLUTE, SNOUT, *and* STARVELING

QUINCE Have you been to Bottom's house? Has he come
    home yet?

STARVELING He has not been heard from. No doubt he has been
    transported.

FLUTE If he doesn't come, then the play is ruined. It can't   5
    go on, can it?

QUINCE It is not possible. You have not a man in all
    Athens able to portray Pyramus but he.

FLUTE No, he simply has the greatest talent of any handicraft
    man in Athens.   10

QUINCE Yes, and the best appearance too, and he is a very
    paramour of a sweet voice.

FLUTE You must say "paragon." A "paramour" is (God
    bless us) a wicked thing.

Enter SNUG *the joiner*

SNUG Fellows, the Duke is coming from the temple, and   15
    there are two or three more lords and ladies married. If
    our play had been given, our fortunes would have been made.

FLUTE Oh, sweet brave Bottom! So has he lost sixpence a day
    for life. He could not have escaped sixpence a day. If the
    Duke had not given him sixpence a day for playing Pyramus,   20
    I'll be hanged. He would have deserved it. Sixpence a day for
    Pyramus or nothing!

Enter BOTTOM

BOTTOM Where are these lads? Where are these hearts?

QUINCE Bottom! O most courageous day! O most
happy hour!   25

BOTTOM Masters, I am to discourse wonders. But ask me
not what. For if I tell you, I am no true Athenian. I will
tell you everything, right as it fell out.

QUINCE Let us hear, sweet Bottom.

BOTTOM Not a word of me. All that I will tell you is that   30
the Duke hath dined. Get your apparel together, good
strings to your beards, new ribbons to your pumps. Meet
presently at the palace. Every man look o'er his part. For
the short and the long is, our play is preferred. In any
case, let Thisbe have clean linen, and let not him that   35
plays the lion pare his nails, for they shall hang out for
the lion's claws. And, most dear actors, eat no onions nor
garlic, for we are to utter sweet breath; and I do not doubt
but to hear them say it is a sweet comedy. No more
words. Away! Go, away!   40

Exit

Enter BOTTOM

BOTTOM   Where are these lads? Where are these hearties?

QUINCE   Bottom! Oh, most courageous day! Oh, most

  happy hour!   25

BOTTOM   Fellows, I could tell you wonders. But ask me

  not what. For if I tell you, I am no true Athenian. I will

  tell you everything, just as it happened.

QUINCE   Let us hear, sweet Bottom.

BOTTOM   Not a word from me. All that I will tell you is that   30

  the Duke has dined. Get your costumes together, good

  strings for your beards, new ribbons for your shoes. Meet

  presently at the palace. Every man look over his part. For

  the long and the short of it is, our play has been selected.

  In any case, let Thisbe have clean clothes, and don't let   35

  whoever plays the lion cut his nails, for they shall

  hang out as lion's claws. And, most dear actors, eat

  no onions or garlic, for we must have sweet breath so

  all will say that it is a delightful comedy. No more

  words. Away! Go, away!   40

All exit

Act Five

Scene 1 [*Athens. The palace of Theseus*]

Enter THESEUS, HIPPOLYTA, PHILOSTRATE, *and* ATTENDANTS

HIPPOLYTA 'Tis strange, my Theseus, that these lovers speak of.

THESEUS More strange than true. I never may believe

These antique fables, nor these fairy toys.

Lovers and madmen have such seething brains,

Such shaping fantasies, that apprehend   5

More than cool reason ever comprehends.

The lunatic, the lover, and the poet,

Are of imagination all compact.

One sees more devils than vast hell can hold:

That is the madman. The lover, all as frantic,   10

Sees Helen's beauty in a brow of Egypt.

The poet's eye, in a fine frenzy rolling,

Doth glance from heaven to earth, from earth to heaven,

And as imagination bodies forth

The forms of things unknown, the poet's pen   15

Turns them to shapes and gives to airy nothing

A local habitation and a name.

Such tricks hath strong imagination

That, if it would but apprehend some joy,

Act Five

Scene 1 [*Athens. The palace of Theseus*]

    Enter THESEUS, HIPPOLYTA, PHILOSTRATE, *and* ATTENDANTS

HIPPOLYTA It's strange, my Theseus, this story the lovers tell.

THESEUS More strange than true. I never can believe

    These fantastic fables or these fairy tales.

    Lovers and madmen have such seething brains,

    Imagine such fancies, and can think up   5

    More than cool reason ever comprehends.

    The lunatic, the lover, and the poet,

    Are all caught up in the imagination.

    One sees more devils than vast hell can hold:

    That is the madman. The lover, just as frantic,   10

    Sees Helen of Troy's beauty in a Gypsy's eyebrow.

    The poet's eye, rolling in a fine frenzy,

    Glances from heaven to earth, from earth to heaven,

    And as imagination gives physical shape to

    The forms of things unknown, the poet's pen   15

    Puts them in writing and gives to airy nothing

    A concrete time and place and name.

    Strong imagination can play such tricks

    That, if it merely thinks of some joy,

It comprehends some bringer of that joy.   20

Or in the night, imagining some fear,

How easy is a bush supposed a bear!

HIPPOLYTA But all the story of the night told over,

And all their minds transfigured so together,

More witnesseth than fancy's images   25

And grows to something of great constancy;

But howsoever, strange and admirable.

    Enter LYSANDER, DEMETRIUS, HERMIA, *and* HELENA

THESEUS Here come the lovers, full of joy and mirth.

Joy, gentle friends! Joy and fresh days of love

Accompany your hearts!   30

LYSANDER More than to us

Wait in your royal walks, your board, your bed!

THESEUS Come now, what masques, what dances shall we have,

To wear away this long age of three hours

Between our after-supper and bedtime?   35

Where is our usual manager of mirth?

What revels are in hand? Is there no play

To ease the anguish of a torturing hour?

Call Philostrate.

PHILOSTRATE Here, mighty Theseus.   40

THESEUS Say, what abridgement have you for this evening?

What masque? What music? How shall we beguile

It then thinks of something to bring it.   20

Or in the night, imagining some fear,

How easily a bush is supposed a bear!

HIPPOLYTA But all the story of the night told over,

And all their minds deluded so together,

More was seen than fanciful images   25

And adds up to something certain;

Anyway, its strange and wonderful.

     Enter LYSANDER, DEMETRIUS, HERMIA, *and* HELENA

THESEUS Here come the lovers, full of joy and mirth.

May joy, gentle friends, joy and new days of love

Be in your hearts!   30

LYSANDER And even more to you

In your royal walks, your table, your bed!

THESEUS Come now, what masques, what dances shall we have,

To pass away this long age of three hours

Between our dessert and bedtime?   35

Where is our usual manager of mirth?

What revels are at hand? Is there no play

To ease the torture of waiting?

Call Philostrate

PHILOSTRATE Here, mighty Theseus.   40

THESEUS Say, what pastime have you for this evening?

What masque? What music? How shall we while

The lazy time, if not with some delight?

PHILOSTRATE   There is a brief how many sports are ripe.

    Make a choice of which your Highness will see first.   45

[*Handing him a paper*]

THESEUS   [*reading*] "The battle with the Centaurs, to be sung

    By an Athenian eunuch to the harp."

    We'll none of that. That have I told my love

    In glory of my kinsman Hercules.

    "The riot of the tipsy Bacchanals,   50

    Tearing the Thracian singer in their rage."

    That is an old device, and it was played

    When I from Thebes came last a conqueror.

    "The thrice-three Muses mourning for the death

    Of learning, late deceased in beggary."   55

    That is some satire, keen and critical,

    Not sorting with a nuptial ceremony.

    "A tedious brief scene of young Pyramus

    And his love Thisbe; very tragical mirth."

    "Merry" and "tragical"? "Tedious" and "brief"?   60

    That is hot ice and wondrous strange snow.

    How shall we find the concord of this discord?

PHILOSTRATE   A play there is, my lord, some ten words long

    (Which is as brief as I have known a play),

    But by ten words, my lord, it is too long,   65

    Which makes it tedious; for in all the play,

    There is not one word apt, one player fitted.

Away the slow time, if not with some delight?

PHILOSTRATE   Here is a list of plays that are ready.

Make a choice of that which your Highness will see first.   45

[*Handing him a paper*]

THESEUS   [*reading*] "The Battle with the Centaurs, to be sung

By an Athenian eunuch at the harp."

We'll have none of that. I've already told the story to my love,

In honor of my kinsman Hercules.

"The Riot of the Tipsy Bacchanals,   50

Tearing the Thracian Singer in Their Rage."

That is an old one, and it was performed

When I last came from Thebes as a conqueror.

"The thrice-three Muses mourning for the death

Of learning, late deceased in beggary."   55

That is some keen and critical satire,

But not right for a wedding ceremony.

"A tedious brief scene of young Pyramus

And his love Thisbe, very tragical mirth."

"Merry" and "tragical"? "Tedious" and "brief"?   60

That is hot ice and very odd snow.

How can we reconcile these opposites?

PHILOSTRATE   It is a play, my lord, some ten words long,

Which is as brief as I have known a play;

But, my lord, it is ten words too long,   65

Which makes it tedious; for in all the play

There is not one apt word, one suitable player.

And tragical, my noble lord, it is.

For Pyramus therein doth kill himself,

Which, when I saw rehearsed, I must confess,   70

Made mine eyes water; but more merry tears

The passion of loud laughter never shed.

THESEUS   What are they that do play it?

PHILOSTRATE   Hard-handed men that work in Athens here,

Which never labored in their minds till now,   75

And now have toiled their unbreathed memories

With this same play, against your nuptial.

THESEUS   And we will hear it.

PHILOSTRATE   No, my noble lord.

It is not for you. I have heard it over,   80

And it is nothing, nothing in the world,

Unless you can find sport in their intents,

Extremely stretched and conned with cruel pain,

To do you service.

THESEUS   I will hear that play,   85

For never anything can be amiss

When simpleness and duty tender it.

Go bring them in; and take your places, ladies.

                                        Exit PHILOSTRATE

HIPPOLYTA   I love not to see wretchedness o'ercharged,

And duty in his service perishing.   90

THESEUS   Why, gentle sweet, you shall see no such thing.

And tragical, my noble lord, it is.

For in it Pyramus does kill himself.

Which, when I saw it rehearsed, I must confess,   70

Brought tears to my eyes; but more merry tears

Than a fit of loud laughter ever caused.

THESEUS Who are they who act in it?

PHILOSTRATE Callous-handed men who work in Athens,

Who never worked with their minds till now;   75

And now have labored with untrained memories

To present this play for your wedding.

THESEUS And we will hear it.

PHILOSTRATE No, my noble lord;

It is not for you. I have heard it done,   80

And it is a trifle, a waste of your time,

Unless you are amused by their attempt.

They have worked hard and memorized with care,

To pay you honor.

THESEUS I will hear that play,   85

For something can never be wrong

When simpleness and duty offer it.

Go, bring them in; and take your places, ladies.

Exit PHILOSTRATE

HIPPOLYTA I do not like to see poor people overburdened,

And failing in their efforts to please a superior.   90

THESEUS Why, gentle sweet, you shall see no such thing.

HIPPOLYTA He says they can do nothing in this kind.
THESEUS The kinder we, to give them thanks for nothing.
      Our sport shall be to take what they mistake;
      And what poor duty cannot do, noble respect   95
      Takes it in might, not merit.
      Where I have come, great clerks have purposed
      To greet me with premeditated welcomes,
      Where I have seen them shiver and look pale,
      Make periods in the midst of sentences,   100
      Throttle their practiced accent in their fears,
      And, in conclusion, dumbly have broke off,
      Not paying me a welcome. Trust me, sweet,
      Out of this silence yet I picked a welcome,
      And in the modesty of fearful duty,   105
      I read as much from the rattling tongue
      Of saucy and audacious eloquence.
      Love, therefore, and tongue-tied simplicity
      In least speak most, to my capacity.
                  Enter PHILOSTRATE
PHILOSTRATE So please your Grace, the Prologue is addressed.   110
THESEUS Let him approach.
Flourish of trumpets. Enter the PROLOGUE (QUINCE)
PROLOGUE If we offend, it is with our good will.
      That you should think, we come not to offend,
      But with good will. To show our simple skill,
      That is the true beginning of our end.   115

HIPPOLYTA He says they can do nothing of this kind.

THESEUS The kinder we are to thank them for nothing.

    Our fun shall be to see where they make mistakes;

    And when their poor effort fails, our nobility   95

    Will appreciate the effort made.

    When I travel, scholars have intended

    To greet me with rehearsed welcomes,

    But I have seen them shiver and grow pale,

    Put periods in the middle of sentences,   100

    Choke on their practiced delivery in their fears,

    And, in conclusion, break off in silence,

    Not giving me a welcome. Trust me, sweet,

    Out of their silence I understood a welcome;

    And in their shyness at such responsibility,   105

    I read as much as from some rattling tongue

    That spoke with bold and daring eloquence.

    Love, therefore, and tongue-tied simplicity

    Speak most, as far as I'm concerned.

                 Enter PHILOSTRATE

PHILOSTRATE If it please your Grace, the Prologue is ready.   110

THESEUS Let him approach.

[*Trumpet fanfare. Enter* PROLOGUE (QUINCE)]

PROLOGUE If we offend, it is with our good will.

    That you should think, we come not to offend,

    But with good will. To show our simple skill,

    That is the true beginning of our end.   115

Consider then, we come but in despite.
We do not come, as minding to content you,
Our true intent is. All for your delight,
We are not here. That you should here repent you,
The actors are at hand; and, by their show,   120
You shall know all, that you are like to know.

Exits

THESEUS This fellow doth not stand upon points.

LYSANDER He hath rid his prologue like a rough colt; he
knows not the stop. A good moral, my lord: it is not
enough to speak, but to speak true.   125

HIPPOLYTA Indeed he hath played on his prologue like a child
on a recorder—a sound, but not in government.

THESEUS His speech was like a tangled chain—nothing impaired,
but all disordered. Who is next?

Enter PYRAMUS, THISBE, WALL, MOONSHINE, LION, *and* PROLOGUE

PROLOGUE Gentles, perchance you wonder at this show.   130
But wonder on, till truth make all things plain.
This man is Pyramus, if you would know.
This beauteous lady Thisbe is certain.
This man, with lime and roughcast, doth present
"Wall," that vile wall which did these lovers sunder;   135
And through Wall's chink, poor souls, they are content
To whisper. At the which let no man wonder.
This man, with lantern, dog, and bush of thorn,
Presenteth "Moonshine," for, if you will know,

Consider then, we come but not in spite.

We do not come, as meaning to please you,

Our true intent is. All for your delight,

We are not here. That you're sorry you've seen our play, too,

The actors are at hand: and, by their show,   120

You shall know all, that you are likely to know.

Exits

THESEUS This fellow isn't fussy about punctuation.

LYSANDER He rode his prologue like a rough colt; he

doesn't know how to stop a sentence. A good moral,

my lord: It's not enough to speak, one must speak correctly.   125

HIPPOLYTA Indeed he has played on his prologue like a child

on a flute—a sound but uncontrolled.

THESEUS His speech was like a tangled chain—nothing broken,

but all out of order. Who is next?

Enter PYRAMUS, THISBE, WALL, MOONSHINE, LION, *and* PROLOGUE

PROLOGUE Gentlefolk, perhaps you are amazed at this show.   130

But keep wondering, till truth makes all things plain.

This man is Pyramus, if you'd like to know.

This beautiful lady, Thisbe, that's certain

This man, with lime and plaster, does present

"Wall," vile wall that keeps these lovers separate;   135

And through Wall's chink, poor souls, they are content

To whisper. So don't be surprised or wonder.

This man—with lantern, dog, and thorny bush—

Presents "Moonshine," for, you need to know,

By moonshine did these lovers think no scorn   140
To meet at Ninus' tomb, there, there to woo.
This grisly beast, which Lion hight by name,
The trusty Thisbe, coming first by night,
Did scare away, or rather did affright;
And as she fled, her mantle she did fall,   145
Which Lion vile with bloody mouth did stain.
Anon comes Pyramus, sweet youth and tall,
And finds his trusty Thisbe's mantle slain.
Whereat, with blade, with bloody blameful blade,
He bravely broached his boiling bloody breast.   150
And Thisbe, tarrying in mulberry shade,
His dagger drew, and died. For all the rest,
Let Lion, Moonshine, Wall, and lovers twain
At large discourse while here they do remain.

THESEUS I wonder if the lion be to speak.   155

DEMETRIUS No wonder, my lord. One lion may, when many
        asses do.

        Exit PROLOGUE, PYRAMUS, LION, THISBE, *and* MOONSHINE

WALL (SNOUT) In this same interlude it doth befall
        That I, one Snout by name, present a wall;
        And such a wall, as I would have you think,   160
        That had in it a crannied hole or chink;
        Through which the lovers, Pyramus and Thisbe,
        Did whisper often, very secretly.
        This loam, this roughcast, and this stone doth show
        That I am that same wall. The truth is so.   165
        And this the cranny is, right and sinister,

By moonshine were these lovers not too proud   140
To meet at Ninus' tomb, and there to woo.
This gruesome beast, a lion is, that's right.
Faithful Thisbe, who arrived first that night,
Did scare away, or frighten into flight;
And as she fled, her cloak she let fall,   145
Which Lion vile with bloody mouth did stain.
And then comes Pyramus, sweet youth and tall,
And finds his faithful Thisbe's cloak slain,
At that, with blade, with bloody blameful blade
He bravely broke his boiling bloody breast.   150
And Thisbe, waiting in the mulberry's shade,
His dagger drew and died. For all the rest—
Let Lion, Moonshine, Wall, and loving pair
Explain in full while they linger here.

THESEUS I wonder if the lion will speak.   155
DEMETRIUS Don't wonder, my lord. One lion may, when many
            asses do.

            Exit PROLOGUE, PYRAMUS, LION, THISBE, *and* MOONSHINE

WALL (SNOUT) In this same little play you will recall
            That I, one Snout by name, portray a wall;
            And such a wall as I would have you think,   160
            That had in it a cranny, hole, or chink;
            Through which the lovers, Pyramus and Thisbe,
            Could whisper often, very secretly.
            This clay, this plaster, and this stone all show
            That I am that very wall. It is so.   165
            And this is the hole, running right and left,

Through which the fearful lovers are to whisper.

THESEUS Would you desire lime and hair to speak better?

DEMETRIUS It is the wittiest partition that ever I heard

    discourse, my lord.   170

Enter PYRAMUS

THESEUS Pyramus draws near the wall. Silence!

PYRAMUS (BOTTOM) O grim-looked night! O night with hue so black!

    O night, which ever art when day is not!

    O night, O night! Alack, alack, alack!

    I fear my Thisbe's promise is forgot!   175

    And thou, O wall, O sweet, O lovely wall,

    That stand'st between her father's ground and mine,

    Thou wall, O sweet and lovely wall,

    Show me thy chink, to blink through with mine eyne!

[WALL *holds up his fingers*]

    Thanks, courteous wall; Jove shield thee well for this.   180

    But what see I? No Thisbe do I see.

    O wicked wall, through whom I see no bliss,

    Cursed be thy stones for thus deceiving me!

THESEUS The wall, methinks, being sensible, should

    curse again.   185

PYRAMUS No, in truth, sir, he should not. "Deceiving me"

    is Thisbe's cue. She is to enter now, and I am to spy her

    through the wall. You shall see it will fall pat as I told

    you. Yonder she comes.

Through which the anxious lovers whisper, like a theft.

THESEUS Would you ask for lime and hair to speak better?

DEMETRIUS It is the wittiest partition that I ever heard

    speak, my lord.   170

Enter PYRAMUS

THESEUS Pyramus draws near the wall. Silence!

PYRAMUS Oh, grim-faced night! Oh, night with hue so black!

    Oh, night that always is when day is not!

    Oh night, oh night! Alack, alack, alack,

    I fear my Thisbe's promise is forgot!   175

    And you, Oh, wall, Oh, sweet, Oh, lovely wall,

    That between her father's land and mine lies!

    You, wall, Oh, sweet and lovely wall,

    Show me the chink, to glance through with my eyes

[WALL *holds up his fingers*]

    Thanks courteous wall, Jove protect you well for this.   180

    What do I see? No Thisbe do I see.

    Oh, wicked wall, through whom I see no bliss,

    Cursed be your stones for so deceiving me!

THESEUS Since the wall has feelings I think it should

    curse back.   185

PYRAMUS No, in truth, sir, he should not. "Deceiving me"

    is Thisbe's cue. She should enter now, and I am to spy her

    through the wall. You shall see it will turn out just as I told

    you. Here she comes now.

Enter THISBE

THISBE (FLUTE) O wall, full often hast thou heard my moans   190
    For parting my fair Pyramus and me!
    My cherry lips have often kissed thy stones,
    Thy stones with lime and hair knit up in thee.

PYRAMUS I see a voice. Now will I to the chink,
    To spy an I can hear my Thisbe's face.   195
    Thisbe!

THISBE My love! Thou art my love, I think.

PYRAMUS Think what thou wilt, I am thy lover's grace,
    And, like Limander, am I trusty still.

THISBE And I, like Helen, till the Fates me kill.   200

PYRAMUS Not Shafalus to Procrus was so true.

THISBE As Shafalus to Procrus, I to you.

PYRAMUS O, kiss me through the hole of this vile wall!

THISBE I kiss the wall's hole, not your lips at all.

PYRAMUS Wilt thou at Ninny's tomb meet me straightway?   205

THISBE 'Tide life, 'tide death, I come without delay.

                                    Exit PYRAMUS *and* THISBE

WALL Thus have I, Wall, my part discharged so,
    And, being done, thus Wall away doth go.

                                         Exit WALL

THESEUS Now is the wall down between the two
    neighbors.   210

DEMETRIUS No remedy, my lord, when walls are so wilful to
    hear without warning.

Enter THISBE

THISBE (FLUTE) Oh wall, how often you have heard my moans   190
    For parting fair Pyramus and me there
    My cherry lips have often kissed your stones,
    Your stones all mixed with lime and hair.

PYRAMUS I see a voice. Now I'll look through the chink,
    To spy, and I can hear my Thisbe's face.   195
    Thisbe!

THISBE My love! You are my love, I think.

PYRAMUS Think what you will, I am your lover's grace;
    And, like Limander, am faithful still.

THISBE And I, like Helen, till the Fates me kill.   200

PYRAMUS Not Shafalus to Procrus was so true.

THISBE As Shafalus to Procrus, so am I to you.

PYRAMUS Oh, kiss me though the hole of this worthless wall!

THISBE I kiss the wall's hole, not your lips at all.

PYRAMUS Will you meet me at Ninny's tomb straightaway?   205

THISBE Come life, come death, I leave without delay

                           Exit PYRAMUS *and* THISBE

WALL So, I, Wall, have discharged my part so;
    And, being done, as Wall, away I go.

                                  Exit WALL

THESEUS Now the wall is down between the two
    neighbors.   210

DEMETRIUS That won't help, my lord, when walls have minds
    of their own and listen when you least expect it.

HIPPOLYTA   This is the silliest stuff that ever I heard.

THESEUS   The best in this kind are but shadows; and the

    worst are no worse, if imagination amend them.   215

HIPPOLYTA   It must be your imagination, then, and not theirs.

THESEUS   If we imagine no worse of them than they of

    themselves, they may pass for excellent men. Here come

    two noble beasts in, a man and a lion.

Enter LION *and* MOONSHINE

LION (SNUG) You, ladies, you whose gentle hearts do fear   220

    The smallest monstrous mouse that creeps on floor,

    May now, perchance, both quake and tremble here,

    When lion rough in wildest rage doth roar.

    Then know that I, as Snug the joiner am,

    A lion-fell, nor else no lion's dam;   225

    For, if I should as lion come in strife

    Into this place, 'twere pity on my life.

THESEUS   A very gentle beast, and of a good conscience.

DEMETRIUS   The very best at a beast, my lord, that e'er I saw.

LYSANDER   This lion is a very fox for his valor.   230

THESEUS   True, and a goose for his discretion.

DEMETRIUS   Not so, my lord, for his valor cannot carry his

    discretion, and the fox carries the goose.

THESEUS   His discretion, I am sure, cannot carry his valor,

    for the goose carries not the fox. It is well. Leave it to his   235

    discretion, and let us listen to the moon.

HIPPOLYTA   This is the silliest stuff I ever heard.

THESEUS   The best plays are only shadows of life; and the
    worst are no worse, if imagination is used.   215

HIPPOLYTA   It must be your imagination, then, and not theirs.

THESEUS   If we imagine as well of them as they do of
    themselves, they'll pass for excellent actors. Here come
    two noble beasts, a man and a lion.

                Enter LION and MOONSHINE

LION (SNUG)   You ladies, you whose gentle hearts do fear   220
    The smallest frightful mouse that creeps on floor,
    May now perhaps both quake and tremble here,
    When rough lion in wildest rage does roar.
    Then know that I, one Snug the joiner, be
    A lionskin, not even a lioness in reality;   225
    For, if I should, like a lion, come as an enemy
    Into this place, it would disgrace every part of me.

THESEUS   A very polite beast, and considerate, too.

DEMETRIUS   The best at a beast, my lord, I ever saw.

LYSANDER   This lion, as far as courage goes, is a true fox.   230

THESEUS   True, and as far as sense goes, a goose.

DEMETRIUS   Not so, my lord, for his courage is too weak for his
    caution, but a fox can overcome a goose.

THESEUS   His sense, I am sure, is no stronger than his courage,
    for the goose can't overcome the fox. All right. We'll   235
    leave it to him, and let us listen to the moon.

MOONSHINE (STARVELING) This lanthorn doth the horned moon present—
DEMETRIUS He should have worn the horns on his head.
THESEUS He is no crescent, and his horns are invisible
    within the circumference. 240
MOONSHINE This lanthorn doth the horned moon present.
    Myself the man i' the moon do seem to be.
THESEUS This is the greatest error of all the rest. The man
    should be put into the lanthorn. How is it else the man
    in the moon? 245
DEMETRIUS He dares not come there, for the candle; for, you
    see, it is already in snuff.
HIPPOLYTA I am aweary of this moon. Would he would
    change!
THESEUS It appears, by his small light of discretion, that he 250
    is in the wane; but yet, in courtesy, in all reason, we must
    stay the time.
LYSANDER Proceed, Moon.
MOONSHINE All that I have to say is to tell you that the
    lanthorn is the moon. I, the man in the moon; this thornbush, 255
    my thornbush; and this dog, my dog.
DEMETRIUS Why, all these should be in the lanthorn; for all
    these are in the moon. But silence! Here comes Thisbe.

                      Enter THISBE

MOONSHINE (STARVELING) This lantern represents the horned moon—

DEMETRIUS He should have worn the horns on his head.

THESEUS He is a round, full moon, and so his horns are invisible

    within the circumference.   240

MOONSHINE This lantern represents the horned moon.

    And it seems I'm the man in the moon.

THESEUS This is the greatest error of all. The man

    should be put into the lantern. How else can he be

    the man in the moon?   245

DEMETRIUS He dares not go there because of the candle; for, you see,

    it is already smoking.

HIPPOLYTA I'm tired of this moon. I wish he would

    change!

THESEUS It appears from the dimness of his light, that he   250

    is on the wane; but yet, in courtesy and fairness, we must

    wait out the time.

LYSANDER Proceed, Moon.

MOONSHINE All that I have to say is to tell you that the

    lantern is the moon. I'm the man in the moon. This thornbush   255

    is my thornbush, and this dog, my dog

DEMETRIUS Why then, all these should be in the lantern, for all

    these are in the moon. But silence! Here comes Thisbe.

Enter THISBE

THISBE   This is old Ninny's tomb. Where is my love?

LION [*Roars*]   O!   260

> *Exit* THISBE, *running*

DEMETRIUS   Well roared, Lion!

THESEUS   Well run, Thisbe!

HIPPOLYTA   Well shone, Moon! Truly, the moon shines with a
good grace.

> [LION *tears* THISBE'S *mantle and exits*]

THESEUS   Well moused, Lion!   265

DEMETRIUS   And then came Pyramus.

LYSANDER   And so the lion vanished.

> *Enter* PYRAMUS

PYRAMUS   Sweet moon, I thank thee for thy sunny beams;
I thank thee, moon, for shining now so bright;
For, by thy gracious, golden, glittering gleams,   270
I trust to take of truest Thisbe sight.
But stay! O spite!
But mark, poor knight!
What dreadful dole is here?
Eyes, do you see?   275
How can it be?
O dainty duck! O dear!
Thy mantle good,
What, stained with blood?
Approach, ye Furies fell!   280
O Fates, come, come!
Cut thread, and thrum,
Quail, crush, conclude, and quell!

THISBE This is old Ninny's tomb. Where is my love?

LION [*Roars*] Oh!   260

Exit THISBE, running

DEMETRIUS Well roared, Lion!

THESEUS Well run, Thisbe!

HIPPOLYTA Well shone, Moon! Truly the moon does shine
  gracefully.

[LION tears THISBE'S cloak and exits]

THESEUS Well moused, Lion!   265

DEMETRIUS And now comes Pyramus.

LYSANDER And so the lion vanishes.

Enter PYRAMUS

PYRAMUS Sweet moon, I thank you for your sunny beams;
  I thank you, Moon, for shining now so bright;
  For by your gracious, golden, glittering gleams,   270
  I hope to take of truest Thisbe sight.
          But wait! Oh spite!
          But look, poor knight!
  What dreadful woe is here?
          Eyes, do you see?   275
          How can it be?
  Oh dainty duck! Oh dear!
          Your good cloak,
          What, stained with blood?
  Approach, cruel Furies!   280
          Oh Fates, come, tread!
          Cut fringe and thread;
  Quell, crush, conclude, and rule!

THESEUS This passion, and the death of a dear friend,

would go near to make a man look sad.   285

HIPPOLYTA Beshrew my heart, but I pity the man.

PYRAMUS O, wherefore, Nature, didst thou lions frame?

Since lion vile hath here deflowered my dear?

Which is—no, no! which was—the fairest dame

That lived, that loved, that liked, that looked with cheer.   290

Come, tears, confound!

Out, sword, and wound

The pap of Pyramus!

Ay, that left pap

Where heart doth hop. [*Stabs himself*]   295

Thus die I, thus, thus, thus.

Now am I dead,

Now am I fled;

My soul is in the sky.

Tongue, lose thy light,   300

Moon, take thy flight.

Exit MOONSHINE

Now die, die, die, die, die! [*He dies*]

DEMETRIUS No die, but an ace, for him; for he is but one.

LYSANDER Less than an ace, man, for he is dead, he is

nothing.   305

THESEUS With the help of a surgeon, he might yet recover,

and yet prove an ass.

THESEUS This passion, and the death of a dear friend,

    would almost make a man feel sad.   285

HIPPOLYTA Curse my heart, but I pity the man.

PYRAMUS Oh, why, Nature did you a lion devise?

    Since this vile lion has killed my dear?

    Who is—no, no! who was—the fairest prize

    That lived, that loved, that liked, that looked with cheer.   290

        Come tears, defeat!

        Out, sword, and meet

    The breast of Pyramus!

        Ay, that left breast

        Where heart does rest. [*Stabs himself*]   295

    Thus die I, thus, thus, thus.

        Now I am dead,

        Now I am fled;

    My soul is in the sky.

        Tongue, lose your light,   300

        Moon, now take flight.

                  Exit MOONSHINE

    Now die, die, die, die, die! [*He dies*]

DEMETRIUS He's rolled the least score on the die—an ace, just one!

LYSANDER Less than an ace, man; for, being dead, he is

    nothing.   305

THESEUS With the help of a surgeon he might recover yet

    and still prove an ass.

HIPPOLYTA How chance Moonshine is gone before Thisbe
 comes back and finds her lover?

THESEUS She will find him by starlight. Here she comes;   310
 and her passion ends the play.

Enter THISBE

HIPPOLYTA Methinks she should not use a long one for such a
 Pyramus. I hope she will be brief.

DEMETRIUS A mote will turn the balance, which Pyramus,
 which Thisbe, is the better; he for a man, God warrant 315
 us!—she for a woman, God bless us!

LYSANDER She has spied him already with those sweet eyes.

DEMETRIUS And thus she means, *videlicet*—

THISBE Asleep, my love?

   What, dead, my dove?   320

O Pyramus, arise!

   Speak, speak! Quite dumb?

   Dead? Dead? A tomb

Must cover thy sweet eyes.

   These lily lips,   325

   This cherry nose,

These yellow cowslip cheeks,

   Are gone, are gone.

   Lovers, make moan!

His eyes were green as leeks.   330

   O Sisters Three

HIPPOLYTA How is it Moonshine has gone before Thisbe
    comes back and finds her lover?

THESEUS She will find him by starlight. Here she comes;   310
    and her show of sorrow ends the play.

Enter THISBE

HIPPOLYTA I think she should not have a long one for such a
    Pyramus. I hope she will be brief.

DEMETRIUS A speck could turn the balance of which is the better
    character, Pyramus or Thisbe. He as a man, God help us!—   315
    or she as a woman, God bless us!

LYSANDER She has spied him already with those sweet eyes.

DEMETRIUS And so she complains, as follows:

THISBE   Asleep, my love?

      What, dead, my dove?   320

Oh, Pyramus, arise!

      Speak, speak! Quite dumb?

      Dead, dead? A tomb

Must cover your sweet eyes.

      These lily lips,   325

      This cherry nose,

These yellow cowslip cheeks,

      Are gone, are gone.

      Lovers, make moan!

His eyes were green as leeks.   330

      Oh, Furies three,

Come, come to me,
With hands as pale as milk.
Lay them in gore,
Since you have shore   335
With shears his thread of silk.
Tongue, not a word!
Come, trusty sword;
Come, blade, my breast imbrue! [*Stabs herself*]
And farewell, friends.   340
Thus Thisbe ends.
Adieu, adieu, adieu! [*Dies*]

THESEUS Moonshine and Lion are left to bury the dead.

DEMETRIUS Ay, and Wall too.

BOTTOM [*Starts up*] No, I assure you; the wall is down that   345
parted their fathers. Will it please you to see the Epilogue,
or to hear a Bergomask dance between two of our
company?

THESEUS No epilogue, I pray you. For your play needs no
excuse. Never excuse. For when the players are all dead,   350
there need none to be blamed. Marry, if he that writ it
had played Pyramus and hanged himself in Thisbe's
garter, it would have been a fine tragedy; and so it is,
truly, and very notably discharged. But, come, your
Bergomask. Let your epilogue alone.   355

[*Dance, and the players exit*]

Come, come to me,
With hands as pale as bread;
Lay them in gore,
Since you have shorn,   335
With shears his life's thread.
Tongue, not a word!
Come, trusty sword;
Come, blade, my breast now try! [*Stabs herself*]
And farewell, friends.   340
Thus Thisbe ends.
Goodbye, goodbye, goodbye! [*She dies*]

THESEUS Moonshine and Lion are left to bury the dead.

DEMETRIUS Yes, and Wall too.

BOTTOM [*Jumps up*] No, I assure you; the wall is down that   345
parted their fathers. Would you like to see the Epilogue,
or to hear a Bergomask dance between two of our
company?

THESEUS No epilogue, I beg you. For your play needs no
excuses. Never apologize. For when all the players are dead,   350
there's no need to blame anyone. You know, if the writer
had played Pyramus and hanged himself in Thisbe's
garter, it would have been a fine tragedy; and it has
truly been so, and very well performed. But, come, your
Bergomask! Never mind your Epilogue.   355

[*A comic country dance as the players exit*]

The iron tongue of midnight hath told twelve.

Lovers, to bed. 'Tis almost fairy time.

I fear we shall outsleep the coming morn

As much as we this night have overwatched.

This palpable gross play hath well beguiled 360

The heavy gait of night. Sweet friends, to bed.

A fortnight hold we this solemnity

In nightly revels and new jollity.

Exit all

Enter PUCK

PUCK Now the hungry lion roars,

      And the wolf behowls the moon, 365

Whilst the heavy ploughman snores,

      All with weary task fordone.

Now the wasted brands do glow,

      Whilst the screech owl, screeching loud,

Puts the wretch that lies in woe 370

      In remembrance of a shroud.

Now it is the time of night

      That the graves, all gaping wide,

Every one lets forth his sprite

      In the churchyard paths to glide. 375

And we fairies, that do run

      By the triple Hecate's team

From the presence of the sun,

      Following darkness like a dream,

Now are frolic. Not a mouse 380

Shall disturb this hallowed house.

I am sent with broom before

To sweep the dust behind the door.

The bell has tolled twelve strokes for midnight.

Lovers, to bed. It's almost fairy time.

I'm afraid we'll oversleep in the morning

Just as we've stayed up late tonight.

This terribly silly play has well whiled away   360

The long evening. Sweet friends, to bed.

For two weeks we'll continue festivities

With nightly revels and new jollities.

Exit all

Enter PUCK

PUCK   Now the hungry lion roars,

      And the wolf howls at the moon,   365

While the hearty ploughman snores,

      With all his heavy tasks now done.

Now the burned up coals glow still,

      While the screech owl, screeching loud,

Puts the wretch that lies so ill   370

      In mind of a burial shroud.

Now it is the time of night

      That the graves, all gaping wide,

Every one lets out its sprite,

      In the churchyard paths to glide.   375

And we fairies, who do run

      As members of Diana's team

From the presence of the sun,

      Following darkness like a dream,

Now do frolic. Not a mouse   380

Shall disturb this blessed house.

I am sent with broom before,

To sweep the dust behind the door.

Enter TITANIA *and* OBERON *and their trains*

OBERON   Through the house give glimmering light,

      By the dead and drowsy fire.   385

  Every elf and fairy sprite

      Hop as light as bird from briar,

  And this ditty, after me,

  Sing, and dance it trippingly.

TITANIA   First rehearse your song by rote,   390

  To each word a warbling note.

  Hand in hand, with fairy grace,

  Will we sing and bless this place.

[*Song and dance*]

OBERON   Now until the break of day,

  Through this house each fairy stray.   395

  To the best bride-bed will we,

  Which by us shall blessed be,

  And the issue there create

  Ever shall be fortunate.

  So shall all the couples three   400

  Ever true in loving be,

  And the blots of Nature's hand

  Shall not in their issue stand,

  Never mole, harelip, nor scar,

  Not mark prodigious, such as are   405

  Despised in nativity,

  Shall upon their children be.

Enter TITANIA, OBERON, *and their attendants*

OBERON   Through the house give glimmering light,

> By the dead and drowsy fire.   385

> Every elf and fairy sprite

> > Hop as light as bird from briar;

> And this tune, now after me,

> Sing and dance it merrily.

TITANIA   First rehearse your song by rote,   390

> Make each word a warbling note.

> Hand in hand, with fairy grace,

> We will sing, and bless this place.

[OBERON *leads the* FAIRIES *in song and dance*]

OBERON   Now until the break of day,

> Through this house each fairy stray.   395

> To the best bride-bed go we,

> Which by us shall blessed be;

> And the children they create

> Ever shall be fortunate.

> So shall all the couples three   400

> Ever true in loving be,

> And no physical deformity

> Ever in their children see.

> Never mole, harelip, nor scar,

> No birthmarks, such as are   405

> Despised in nativity,

> Shall upon their children be.

With this field-dew consecrate,
Every fairy take his gait,
And each several chamber bless, 410
Through this palace, with sweet peace.
And the owner of it blest,
Ever shall in safety rest.
Trip away. Make no stay.
Meet me all by break of day. 415

Exit all but PUCK

PUCK If we shadows have offended,
Think but this, and all is mended—
That you have but slumbered here
While these visions did appear.
And this weak and idle theme, 420
No more yielding but a dream,
Gentles, do not reprehend.
If you pardon, we will mend.
And, as I am an honest Puck,
If we have unearned luck 425
Now to scape the serpent's tongue,
We will make amends ere long;
Else the Puck a liar call.
So, good night unto you all.
Give me your hands, if we be friends, 430
And Robin shall restore amends.

Exit

With this field-dew bless the place,
Every fairy keep the pace,
And each several chambers bless,   410
Through this palace, with sweet peace.
And the owner of it blest
Ever shall in safety rest.
Make no pause. Run away.
Meet me all by break of day.   415

Exit all but PUCK

PUCK   If we actors have offended,
Just think this, and all is mended—
That you have but slumbered here
While these visions did appear.
And this light and silly theme,   420
Means no more than just a dream,
Gentles, do not reprehend,
If you'll pardon, we will mend.
And, as I am an honest Puck,
Should we have some unearned luck   425
To escape an audience hissing,
We'll soon amend whatever's missing;
Or else the Puck a liar call.
So, good night unto you all.
Give me applause if we are friends,   430
And Robin will soon make amends.

Exits

Glossary

The following terms are taken from the translation of *A Midsummer Night's Dream*. The scene and line numbers are given in parentheses after the terms, which are listed in the order they first occur.

Act One

Athens   (scene 1, scene description): the capital and cultural center of Greece, named for the goddess Athena

Theseus   (scene 1, line 1): Duke of Athens, a hero of ancient Greek legend, described as the son of Poseidon

Hippolyta   (scene 1, line 1): a queen of the Amazons, a mythical race of women warriors; she was captured by Theseus

Diana   (scene 1, line 91): the moon goddess and a symbol of chastity

first of May   (scene 1, line 169): May Day, a celebration at the start of spring

Cupid   (scene 1, line 172): the son of Venus and the god of love; he is pictured as a child, blindfolded, holding a bow and arrows

Venus   (scene 1, line 174): the goddess of love and beauty

Dido   (scene 1, line 176): Queen of Carthage, deserted by Aeneas

Aeneas   (scene 1, line 177): Trojan hero of Virgil's *Aenead,* legendary founder of Rome

Pyramus and Thisbe   (scene 2, line 11): tragic lovers in an episode of Ovid's *Metamorphose*s

Hercules   (scene 2, line 24): the son of Zeus and Alcmene; a hero of extraordinary strength, he performed twelve seemingly impossible tasks demanded by Zeus' wife Hera

Phoebus' car   (scene 2, line 30): the chariot of the sun god, Phoebus Apollo

bellows-mender   (scene 2, line 36): worker who repairs the apparatus used to draw air through a valve to encourage a fire or to produce music in an organ

tinker   (scene 2, line 55): a mender of pots and pans

joiner   (scene 2, line 58): a cabinet maker

French-crown-color   (scene 2, line 86): golden

Act Two

Puck (scene 1, line 1): a mischievous sprite or goblin

fairy rings (scene 1, line 9): circles of darker grass in a field, thought to be the dancing ground of fairies

changeling (scene 1, line 23): usually, a child left in place of a baby kidnapped by fairies; here it refers to the stolen child

Amazon (scene 1, line 71): a member of a mythical tribe of warrior women; here refers to Hippolyta

Perigenia...Aegle...Ariadne...Antiope (scene 1, lines 79-81): lovers whom Theseus betrayed and deserted

morris board (scene 1, line 99): an area of grass marked out in squares for a popular country game called nine men's morris

Apollo...Daphne (scene 1, line 235): in the story as told by Ovid, the sun god Apollo pursued Daphne who, to escape him, changed into a laurel tree

Philomel (scene 2, line 13): a name for the nightingale, derived from the girl in Greek mythology who had once been changed into a bird

Act Three

Ninus' tomb (scene 1, line 90): according to Ovid's version of the story, the meeting place of Pyramus and Thisbe, Ninus was the legendary founder of the city of Nineveh

cuckoo (scene 1, line 131): the cry of the cuckoo bird is said to be close to the word *cuckold* and therefore a mocking of men with unfaithful wives

Ethiop (scene 2, line 261): a dark-skinned African

Aurora's mate (scene 2, line 405): Cephalus, beloved of Aurora, goddess of the dawn, and a famous hunter with whom Oberon chased game

Act Four

tongs and the bones (scene 1, line 29): primitive musical instruments used in rural areas

Cadmus (scene 1, line 114): legendary founder of the city of Thebes

Crete (scene 1, line 115): a large island in the Mediterranean off the southeastern coast of Greece

Sparta (scene 1, line 116): a city-state in ancient Greece

Thessalian (scene 1, line 124): from Thessaly, a northern part of ancient Greece

sixpence a day (scene 2, line 18): a pension for this sum given by Theseus; for that time, sixpence a day would have been a substantial sum

Act Five

Helen of Troy (scene 1, line 11): queen of Sparta, known for her beauty; her abduction by the Trojan prince Paris led to the Trojan War

masque (scene 1, line 42): a musical play with elaborate scenery put on in noble houses to celebrate a special occasion

Centaurs (scene 1, line 46): creatures of fable, half-man and half-horse

tipsy Bacchanals (scene 1, line 50): wild women who tore Orpheus, the Tracian singer, to pieces when he stumbled on their secret celebration of Bacchus, god of wine

Thebes (scene 1, line 53): an ancient city in east-central Greece

thrice-three Muses (scene 1, line 54): the nine goddesses who inspired the arts and literature

Limander (scene 1, line 199): Bottom confuses two classical lovers: Leander, the beloved of Hero, and Paris the lover of Helen of Troy. Leander swam the Hellespont by night to visit Hero and was drowned

Shafalus (scene 1, line 201): Bottom mistakes the name of Cephalus whose fidelity to his wife Procis (Procrus) was the subject of legend

Furies (scene 1, line 280): creatures in Greek mythology who pursued mortals who offended natural and moral laws

Fates (scene 1, line 281): three goddesses who determined human destiny; one spun the thread of life, one decided on its length, and one cut it

Bergomask (scene 1, line 355): a vigorous dance, so named because of its popularity among the peasants of Bergamo, Italy

A GUIDE TO THE ECONOMICS AND FISCAL PERFORMANCE OF THE FEDERAL GOVERNMENT (1976-2007)

A GUIDE TO THE ECONOMICS AND FISCAL PERFORMANCE OF THE FEDERAL GOVERNMENT (1976-2007)

ROBERT P. SINGII

Nova Science Publishers, Inc.

New York

NOTICE TO THE READER

The Publisher has taken reasonable care in the preparation of this book, but makes no expressed or implied warranty of any kind and assumes no responsibility for any errors or omissions. No liability is assumed for incidental or consequential damages in connection with or arising out of information contained in this book. The Publisher shall not be liable for any special, consequential, or exemplary damages resulting, in whole or in part, from the readers' use of, or reliance upon, this material.

Independent verification should be sought for any data, advice or recommendations contained in this book. In addition, no responsibility is assumed by the publisher for any injury and/or damage to persons or property arising from any methods, products, instructions, ideas or otherwise contained in this publication.

This publication is designed to provide accurate and authoritative information with regard to the subject matter covered herein. It is sold with the clear understanding that the Publisher is not engaged in rendering legal or any other professional services. If legal or any other expert assistance is required, the services of a competent person should be sought. FROM A DECLARATION OF PARTICIPANTS JOINTLY ADOPTED BY A COMMITTEE OF THE AMERICAN BAR ASSOCIATION AND A COMMITTEE OF PUBLISHERS.

LIBRARY OF CONGRESS CATALOGING-IN-PUBLICATION DATA

Singh, Robert P. (Robert Paul), 1969-
A guide to the economics & fiscal performance of the federal government (1976-2007) / Robert P. Singh.
p. cm.
Includes index.
ISBN 978-1-60692-428-0 (softcover)
1. Budget--United States--History. 2. Government spending policy--United States--History. 3. Finance, Public--United States--History. I. Title. II. Title: Guide to the economics and fiscal performance of the federal government.
HJ2051.S495   2009
336.7309'045--dc22   2008044928

Published by Nova Science Publishers, Inc ✦ New York

For my children, Jade and Ajay

CONTENTS

Chapter 1

INTRODUCTION

As Americans, we enjoy the benefits of living in a free and democratic country. But maintaining our freedoms and our democracy requires some effort on the part of the citizenry. We have a basic obligation to be informed about the issues and the actions of our government in order to hold our elected officials accountable for their decisions. Only then can American democracy flourish and continue to pursue the ideals upon which the nation was founded. Unfortunately, the overwhelming majority of us simply do not pay attention to what happens in Washington, and, in many cases, we do not understand how the government operates. This is particularly true when it comes to economic issues and the fiscal performance of the federal government. Most Americans simply do not know such basic financial facts as how much money the U.S. government spends per year, what the national debt is, or how the government covers cash shortfalls that result from deficit spending.

Understanding the economic conditions of the country and the fiscal decisions of the government is critical for two reasons. First, all public policies in the country are subject to economic realities and limitations – the government's resources are considerable, but they are limited by the amount of revenue it generates from taxes and the total amount it can borrow. Just as a household should never spend or borrow money without first knowing what its fiscal position is (i.e., household income, savings, existing debts, etc.), the federal government should operate within its financial means and recognize its fiscal position before spending or borrowing funds to pay for its public policy decisions. Second, the President, Congress, and all agencies of the federal government should be good stewards of American taxpayer money. While there are checks-and-balances within the government, the ultimate check-and-balance mechanism in the U.S. is the election. It is the responsibility of the voters to decide whether our elected leaders have been effective, including whether they have been good financial stewards. We have the power to change our leaders if we determine that they have not met our expectations and their obligations. However, an active, concerned, and well-educated populace is required for representative democracy to work efficiently. There are more people interested in following the latest missing person story that is being covered by the 24-hour cable news channels, or learning the latest gossip about movie stars, or perhaps following a favorite sports team, than knowing what the current account deficit is, where the national debt stands, or how much the government spent on foreign aid programs. Without knowing the economic condition of the country and the implications of the decisions that are made on its behalf, the citizenry cannot properly assess the performance of its elected leaders and thus, cannot hold them accountable.

Perhaps the problem is that the fiscal figures for the government are too large. Some may view the numbers as boring to or too difficult to fully comprehend. Politics contribute to the lack of understanding. We live in a politically-polarized country that is facing challenging economic times. Constant spin from Democratic and Republican leaders infects much of what we hear and read about politics which makes it difficult to know what to believe. Even for those who want to understand the economic implications of the federal government's decisions, the constant spin makes it very difficult to do so. As a result, many people – from members of Congress to average Americans – are confused about fiscal matters. However, fiscal responsibility is not a conservative or liberal ideal – it is a responsibility for all Americans. The reality is that the federal government under both Republican and Democratic presidential administrations and Congresses has engaged in spending habits that have resulted in structural fiscal deficits that have required heavy borrowing in order for the government to function. This has put the nation's economic health at risk. But even more troubling is that the federal government has taken on an enormous amount of debt that is increasingly being held by foreigners. This threatens America's very sovereignty.

The national debt now stands at over $10.5 trillion – a staggering figure that is difficult for most people to truly comprehend. American taxpayers are paying more than $400 billion per year in total interest on that debt, and this figure will only rise in coming years. Even worse, over $2.7 trillion of the national debt is now owed to foreigners, including over $500 billion to China. At the same time, we now import $250 billion more in goods and services from China than we export to China. Taken together, this means that the federal government has implicitly approved an economic policy with respect to China that has us borrowing Chinese money in order to buy Chinese products.

Americans have also increasingly felt the pain at the gas pump, but few realize the true impact of purchasing tens of billions of dollars of oil each month from foreign sources. The rising oil prices and a falling dollar have been primary contributors to the fact that we now owe the Organization of the Petroleum Exporting Countries (OPEC) about $180 billion. The OPEC oil cartel's production decisions have significant impact on world oil prices and the price we pay at the pump. This might not really matter, except that the second largest producer of oil within OPEC is Iran – a nation that is considered an enemy of the U.S. It does not require a Ph.D. in public policy or economics to recognize that the geo-political economic realities of being economically beholden to Iran and China have significant consequences on our government's economic and foreign policy decisions regarding these nations. The fiscal imbalances we have with these countries limit strategic options, because we are financially beholden to them. As a result, they can (and often do) exert great influence on our economy.

Every American should read the U.S. Treasury Department's annual summary of the overall financial conditions surrounding the federal government's spending and revenues. The latest available report, entitled *The Federal Government's Financial Health: A Citizen's Guide to the 2007 Financial Report of the United States Government*[1] provides a very readable, but alarming picture of the fiscal health of the nation. The report clearly establishes that our government's spending priorities and debt accumulation are unsustainable. They will result in a fiscal disaster over the next several decades if action is not taken. Yet, most people either do not know about this report, or do not care enough to read it, let alone consider the implications.

With the enormous national debt and the growing challenges of financing the debt, the increased potential for political influence by foreigners who hold large amounts of American debt, the long-term structural budget deficits that are now in place, and the growing financial strains of popular entitlement programs such as Social Security and Medicare, it is now more important than ever for government officials and policy makers – as well as the voters who must hold them accountable to understand the fiscal environment in which we now find ourselves as a country. The consequences of not dealing with the growing fiscal problems today, while they are manageable, will only serve to worsen the negative effect on future generations of Americans.

---

[1] The report is available online at the U.S. Treasury Department's website at "http://www.fms.treas.gov/frsummary/frsummary2007.pdf" and at the U.S. General Accountability Office's website at "http://www.gao.gov/financial/citizensguide2008.pdf". The full Treasury Department report (2007 Financial Report of the United States Government) is available online at "http://fms.treas.gov/fr/index.html".

The fact that you are reading this book makes clear your interest in government affairs. The purpose of this book is to serve as a reference guide or primer for those who want to better understand the economics of the federal government. Again, the U.S. government has financial limits and it is important for elected politicians who set public policies, students of government, and concerned citizens to understand the realities of these limitations. The chapters that follow provide readers with a straightforward discussion of key economic terms and the fiscal performance of the federal government. No reports or data provided by politically conservative or liberal sources are used. Only objective government statistics kept by federal agencies such as the U.S. Treasury Department, the Congressional Budget Office (CBO), the Bureau of Labor Statistics (BLS), the General Accountability Office (GAO), and the Bureau of Economic Analysis (BEA) are cited throughout the book. Data extracted from these sources are illustrated in easy to understand graphs, charts, and tables so that readers can track the changes over time, as well as compare and contrast economic performance during the presidential administrations from President Jimmy Carter to President George W. Bush.

The book breaks down fiscal performance figures by President as a way to subdivide and compare the U.S. economy during each President's term in office. It should be recognized that Presidents do not fully control the economy. Congress plays an important role in that it approves all spending. However, Presidents have far more influence in setting the nation's economic agenda. They submit the annual budget framework to the Congress before it is approved. They also have the power of the bully pulpit to influence Congress and the American people. Additionally, federal agencies such as the U.S. Treasury Department and the Securities and Exchange Commission – which have enormous power over fiscal policies and regulation over the nation's financial sector – are parts of the Executive Branch of the federal government. Congress provides oversight, but this is often after the fact, when policies and actions have already been taken.

It should also be mentioned that economic policies are implemented differently when one party (Democratic or Republican) controls the White House and both Houses of Congress versus when there is split government. Even the size of the majorities in the House of Representatives and the Senate makes a difference on the dynamics of economic policy making and federal spending. This book does not drill down to that level of analyses. Instead, the focus is on trying to educate the reader on the broader trends in the economy over time.

Chapters 2 through 12 discuss key financial figures (gross domestic product, government spending, deficits, the national debt, etc.). To help readers, and make it easier to understand the numbers, the chapters deliberately follow a similar structure and are consistent in the way the numbers are presented, illustrated, and discussed. Chapter 13 discusses what is known as the "third rail of American politics" – Social Security – and its growing financial instability. Millions of Americans rely on the program for their very survival, but it is unsustainable over the longer term without government intervention and changes to existing laws governing the program. Chapter 14 makes an effort to integrate the numbers and figures from the prior chapters in order to explain what they mean when taken together. It summarizes where the nation is today, from a fiscal standpoint, and outlines several broad needs that must be addressed by policy makers. Chapter 15 provides concluding thoughts.

This book does not try to answer all questions that a reader may have about government finances, nor does it offer specific solutions to the growing fiscal challenges the nation faces. Rather, it provides the reader with information to build a solid foundation and good working knowledge of the federal government's fiscal performance over the last three decades. There is no effort to attempt to influence readers toward any particular solutions. This allows readers to focus on the objective numbers and draw their own conclusions. It is important to cut through the spin and look at the actual figures and raw data related to GDP growth, the national debt, the budget deficits, spending, inflation, unemployment, etc. By looking at the objective economic data and the changes over time, one can gain a better understanding of where we now stand and how we ended up here. Only then, can we hold our leaders responsible for their performance, make educated decisions about what has worked and not worked in the past, and consider options to address our fiscal challenges in the future.

Chapter 2

GROSS DOMESTIC PRODUCT

One of the most widely used measures of how the economy is performing is Gross Domestic Product (GDP). GDP is the total market value – in dollars – of all goods and services produced within the U.S. in a year. GDP does not distinguish between U.S. and foreign-owned companies that produce products or services in the U.S., nor does it include products that are produced by U.S. companies in foreign countries. Thus, it is a great indicator of how well the country's domestic economy is performing because the goods and services it counts are only being produced within the borders of the U.S.[1]

When GDP is rising, the economy is expanding, as the country produces more goods and services within its national borders. When it is rising rapidly – faster than about three percent – then all is usually well economically. More specifically, job growth tends to be strong, unemployment is low, and government revenues increase because as more is produced, there is more that can be taxed. When GDP growth falls below two to three percent, economic concerns grow and Americans start to feel pinched economically. Revenue growth for the government (i.e., tax collections) slows and less money is available to fund existing government programs or to spend on new programs. When GDP contracts for two successive quarters, we have an official recession, and the country feels even more significant economic pain. Obviously, a recession has significant negative impacts on government revenues, and forces elected officials to change government programs, tax policies, and debt accumulation in order to stimulate the economy.

---

[1] For more information about GDP see the U.S. Bureau of Economic Analysis website ("www.bea.gov"). The GDP figures discussed in this book and illustrated in the figures can be found at "http://bea.gov/national/xls/gdplev.xls".

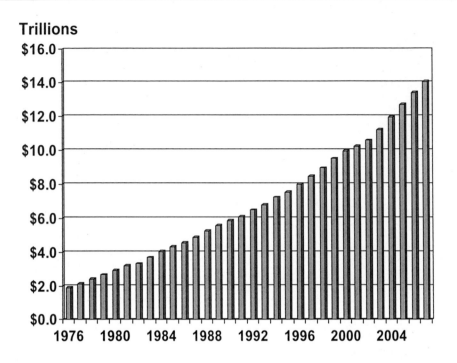

Figure 2-1. U.S. GDP Growth (1976-2007)

The U.S. economy has been resilient and has expanded every year over the last 30 plus years. Figure 2-1 shows the steady growth in U.S. GDP from 1976 to 2007.

In Figure 2-2, we can see that on a dollar basis, the economy has expanded by over $4 trillion over the first seven years of President George W. Bush's term in office. However, even under the four years of the Carter presidency – which has often been maligned as weak economically – U.S. GDP increased by about $1 trillion.

It is important to recognize that a dollar 10 years ago, or 20 years ago, or 30 years ago, is not the same as a dollar in 2008, and the economy is far larger today than it was in the 1970s. For this reason, it is not necessarily surprising that U.S. GDP has grown by the greatest dollar amount in history under the current President relative to prior Presidents.

Trillions

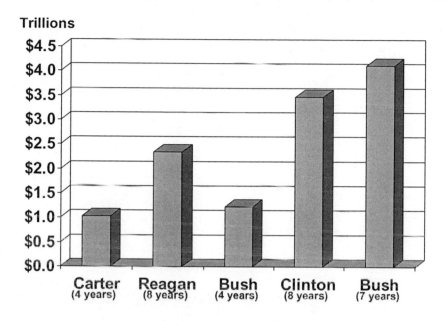

Figure 2-2. Dollar Growth in GDP by President[2]

Consider a household that earns an income of $30,000 (Household A) and a household that earns $200,000 (Household B). It would not be surprising to see Household B grow its household income by more dollars than Household A in a given year. In fact, all other things being equal, we should expect that to happen. However, if the lower income Household A were able to increase income by $20,000 over a four year period (66 percent increase), and Household B increased income by $30,000 over a four-year period (15 percent increase), the increase by Household A would be far more significant and impressive. Even though in terms of actual dollars Household B increased by more than Household A, it is far more difficult to grow income by 66 percent than it is to increase income by 15 percent.

Thus, a better measure of relative performance is how fast and how much the economy grew on a percentage basis over the course of each presidency. For that, we can see in Figure 2-3 that the economy grew by the greatest percentage under President Reagan and grew by the smallest margin under President George H.W. Bush. The eight years of the Reagan presidency saw the economy grow by 80 percent. However, in reality, the economy actually grew faster during the Carter

---

[2] The figures represent the difference between the GDP figures in the final year of each President's term and the final year of the prior President's term. For President George W. Bush, the term is through the fourth quarter of 2007.

presidency. If we divide the total GDP growth by the term length of each President, we can see that during the Carter presidency, GDP grew by an average 13.75 percent per year (55 percent divided by four years), whereas, GDP rose by an average 10 percent per year under Reagan (80 percent divided by eight years).

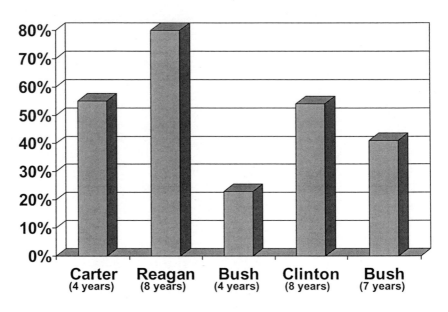

Figure 2-3. Percentage Growth in GDP by President[3]

The actual government GDP figures show that the U.S. economy grew at a healthy pace during each of the last five presidential administrations when you consider the performance over the entire presidencies. This is especially true of the Carter Administration, which again is contrary to the impression many people hold about the economic performance of that presidency.

Obviously, GDP is just one fiscal performance measure. We have to look at other numbers to get a more complete understanding of the financial decisions made by our government and the economic performance of the nation over time and under each President. However, GDP helps us better understand other fiscal performance measures of the government because it provides an important economic context.

---

[3] The figures represent the percentage growth in GDP over the course of each President's term. For President George W. Bush, the term is through the fourth quarter of 2007. Calculated by taking the difference in GDP over the course of each President's term and dividing by the GDP figure at the end of the previous presidency.

To explain how and why, let us consider an example in which GDP is represented as total income in a single household. Let us assume that the total household income is $140,000 per year. The income would be used by the family to address needs and financial priorities. Some money would be spent on daily expenses, some may be put away for retirement, some invested in stocks and mutual funds, some would be used to finance household debt (e.g., car loans, home mortgage, school loans), etc. As income rises, the household must make choices about how to use the additional income. Should it be used to pay down debt? Should the money be saved? Should it be spent? The decision about what to do with the money will be dictated by the goals of the household and the situation it finds itself in. Such is the case with the U.S. government, except instead of making financial decisions based on having $140,000 in household income, the government makes choices based on a figure that includes eight more zeroes – the $14 trillion U.S. GDP.

The above analogy is somewhat imperfect because the government does not have $14 trillion to spend. However, actual government revenues are based on tax collections that are directly tied to U.S. GDP. When GDP is rising rapidly, tax collections tend to rise. Likewise, when GDP is falling, tax revenues tend to fall. With respect to the nation, at different times, different priorities are set. In times of war, more must be spent on defense. When the economy slows, money may be invested in education programs to retrain workers, or it may be used as part of an economic stimulus. However, just as a household must make decisions and choices relative to its own income, the government must consider spending priorities and make economic decisions relative to the GDP. In general, government revenues (i.e., tax collection) should increase at about the same pace as GDP growth, and, in most cases, it is not preferable to increase spending or debt at a faster pace than GDP growth. The reasons for these general "rules of thumb" are explained through examples and discussion in the next several chapters which examine various economic factors and actual financial figures, and compare them back to GDP.

Chapter 3

FEDERAL GOVERNMENT REVENUES

The federal government has to have a source of revenue to generate cash which can be used to pay for government operations and services. While GDP represents the size of the entire U.S. economy, it is not equivalent to government revenues that can be spent on government programs and priorities. It is important for all Americans to understand where the government gets its money (revenue) because the government's money is our money. The primary source of revenue for the government is taxes.

"Tax" is a bad word for many people, but the reality is, through tax revenues the government pays for such things as the military, federal highways, and popular government programs such as Social Security. People may differ on what an appropriate tax burden should be for individuals and corporations (or even whether there should be any taxes whatsoever), but they are a necessary part of American society because they fund our government and the services it provides.

In 2007, the U.S. government collected a record $2.57 trillion in revenues. The sources of the money were as follows:[1]

45% - Individual Income Taxes
14% - Corporate Income Taxes
34% - Social Insurance Taxes
3% - Excise Taxes
1% - Estate and Gift Taxes
1% - Customs Duties
2% - Miscellaneous Receipts

---

[1] Historical revenue collection figures can be found at the Congressional Budget Office website ("www.cbo.gov"). The revenue figures discussed in this book and illustrated in the figures can be found at "http://www.cbo.gov/showdoc.cfm?index=1821&sequence=0".

Clearly, the above figures show that the overwhelming majority of revenues come from individual and corporate income taxes, as well as social insurance taxes. Most Americans are probably familiar with individual income taxes and corporate income taxes, but may not be as clear about what constitutes social insurance taxes. Social insurance taxes are the Federal Insurance Contributions Act (FICA) payroll taxes that are deducted from Americans' paychecks. Currently, they amount to 12.4 percent of gross salary up to $102,000 (no additional FICA taxes are collected for Social Security on salary above $102,000), and 2.9 percent of total gross salary (no limit) for Medicare. These taxes are split evenly between employers and employees. So, while an individual employee making up to $102,000 sees a FICA deduction of 7.65 percent on his/her salary pay stub (6.2 percent for Social Security and 1.45 percent for Medicare), the government also collects 7.65 percent from the employer of that employee. (Additional details about the financial accounting and conditions surrounding Social Security can be found in Chapter 13).

The U.S. government has collected money from the same sources and in largely the same percentages for decades. As a comparison, in 1976, the government collected 44 percent of its revenues from individual income taxes, 14 percent from corporate income taxes, and 30 percent from social insurance taxes. These are fairly consistent with the 2007 figures.

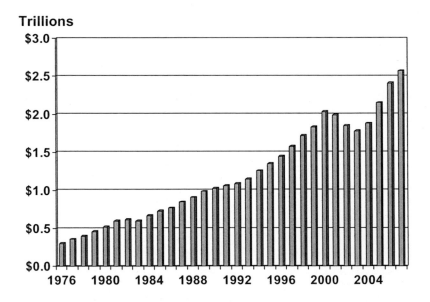

Figure 3-1. Federal Government Revenues (1976-2007)

Figure 3-1 illustrates the annual revenues collected by the U.S. government from 1976 to 2007. Revenues have steadily risen for most of the period. The only major drop in revenues occurred in the early 2000s. These dropping revenues can be attributed to a slowing economy, significant tax cuts, and the September 11 attacks, which had a significant negative economic impact on the country.

Figure 3-2 breaks down the total growth in annual government revenues over the terms of each of the last five Presidents. More specifically, the figures show the difference between how much revenue the government generated at the end of each President's term (e.g., revenues in the final year under President Reagan minus the revenues in the final year of President Carter). By far, annual government revenues increased by the greatest dollar amount during the Clinton presidency. In 1992, the U.S. government generated $1.09 trillion in revenues, but in 2000, the last year of President Clinton's term, government revenues had nearly doubled to $2.03 trillion.

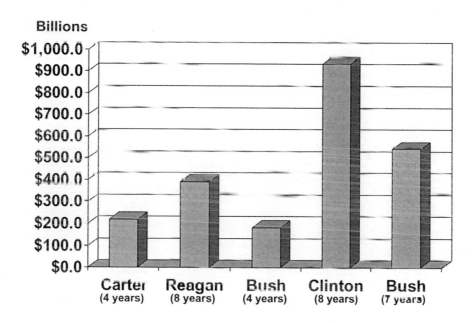

Figure 3-2. Dollar Growth in Annual Government Revenues by President[2]

---

[2] The figures represent the difference between the annual government revenues in the final year of each President's term and the final year of the prior President's term. For President George W. Bush, the term is through the fourth quarter of 2007.

When one looks at the percentage growth in government revenues by President (calculated by taking ending revenue minus starting revenue and dividing the difference by starting revenue), it is clear that Presidents Carter, Reagan, and Clinton saw large percentage gains in revenues during their presidencies (see Figure 3-3). Neither President Bush saw such gains during their presidencies.

Depending on your personal beliefs, growing government revenues may be a good or bad thing. No matter what you believe with respect to growing revenues, it should be recognized that not all growth is the same. If GDP is $1 trillion and the government collects $300 billion in tax revenues, tax revenues would represent 30 percent of GDP ($300 billion/$1 trillion). However, if GDP is $2 trillion and the government collects $500 billion in revenues this would represent 25 percent of GDP ($500 billion/$2 trillion). Thus, even though more taxes were collected in the latter scenario, they were a smaller percentage of total GDP. This would represent a cut in tax rates.

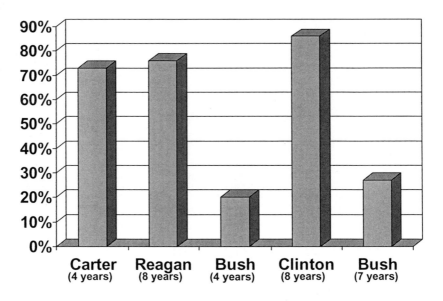

Figure 3-3. Percentage Growth in Annual Government Revenues by President[3]

---

[3] The figures represent the percentage growth in annual revenues over the course of each President's term. For President George W. Bush, the term is through the fourth quarter of 2007. Calculated by taking the difference in annual revenues over the course of each President's term and dividing by the revenues at the end of the previous presidency.

Table 3-1 summarizes the total revenues collected and the GDP figures for the final year of each presidency (2007 figures are shown for President George W. Bush). Then, the revenues as a percentage of GDP are shown in order to allow for some comparison across Presidents. What is clear is that in the final year of President Clinton's term, government revenues were highest as a percentage of the GDP among the last five Presidents.

Table 3-1. Revenue and GDP in the Final Year of Each Presidency[4]

President	Revenues	GDP	Revenues/GDP
Ford	$298 billion	$1.89 trillion	15.8%
Carter	$517 billion	$2.92 trillion	17.7%
Reagan	$909 billion	$5.25 trillion	17.3%
Bush	$1.09 trillion	$6.48 trillion	16.8%
Clinton	$2.03 trillion	$9.95 trillion	20.4%
Bush	$2.57 trillion	$14.07 trillion	18.3%

Finally, Table 3-2 presents a summary of the growth in annual government revenues over the term of each President. For example, under President Carter, the government collected $219 billion more in annual revenues in his last year in office than it did in the last year of the Ford presidency. This represented a 73 percent growth in government revenues. Table 3-2 also summarizes the growth in GDP so that one can see how the revenue growth compared with the GDP growth over the term of each President.

In a world in which nothing changes, we would expect to see revenue growth (or shrinkage) at the same pace as GDP growth (or contraction). But we do not live in such a world and the fact is that things do change – the economy fluctuates, government priorities change, inflation increases and decreases, tax rates change, etc. They all have an impact on how much revenue the government generates. Generally speaking, if you believe that more government programs should be enacted, then you are more likely to want to see greater government revenues to pay for such programs. If you believe the government is too large, you are more likely to want to see government revenues grow at a slower pace or even shrink. Rather than argue about which is better, or advocate one philosophy over another, what is safe to say is that it should be the goal of any politician – liberal or conservative – to ensure that there are enough revenues to cover spending requirements and any new or proposed programs.

---

[4] For the current President Bush, the figures are for the seventh year of his term in office.

Table 3-2. Revenue and GDP Growth by President[5]

President	Annual Gov't Revenues Growth	GDP Growth	% Increase in GDP over Term	% Growth in Annual Gov't Rev. over Term
Carter (4 years)	$219 billion	$1.032 trillion	55%	73%
Reagan (8 years)	$392 billion	$2.337 trillion	80%	76%
Bush (4 years)	$192 billion	$1.230 trillion	23%	20%
Clinton (8 years)	$934 billion	$3.470 trillion	54%	86%
Bush (7 years)	$543 billion	$4.120 trillion	41%	27%

More broadly, in the absence of other information (e.g., government spending, budget deficits, national debt, unemployment, a falling dollar, inflation, etc.), it is impossible to determine if the government is collecting too much, too little, or just enough. Thus, one cannot, and should not, make a determination about which President held office during the best or worst periods of performance fiscal performance based solely on the information contained within Tables 3-1 and 3-2. The revenue information is just one set of numbers and they must be considered in the context of other financial figures. One of these other figures is government spending, which is discussed in the next chapter.

---

[5] The figures represent the difference between the figures in the final year of each President's term and the final year of the prior President's term. For President George W. Bush, the term is through 2007.

Chapter 4

FEDERAL GOVERNMENT SPENDING

One thing that all Americans know is that the federal government spends money. Every year, the President sends a proposed budget to Congress. While the budget provided by the President sets the agenda for government spending, it is not the final budget. Congress debates it and makes changes to the proposed budget, usually adding money for their own priorities. Once both Houses of Congress have passed the budget, they send the approved budget bill to the President who signs it into law or vetoes it. If it is vetoed, Congress can either work with the President to change the bill, or it can overturn the veto by voting to pass the budget over the President's objections. (Overturning a veto requires super majority votes in both the House and Senate.) Once the bill has been signed into law by the President, or Congress overturns a presidential veto, the money for the budget is appropriated (i.e., committed) and the spending begins for the fiscal year. On top of the budgeted amount, supplemental spending bills are approved throughout the year. These spending bills are often needed to cover emergency war funding or federal relief efforts after natural disasters such as tornadoes, floods, or hurricanes.

The end result of all of this spending is that the U.S. government is the single largest customer in the world. It purchases billions of dollars worth of goods and services from private-sector contractors. It is also the largest charity in the world. It pays out billions in foreign and domestic aid programs each year. The taxes and revenues that the government collects and generates are used to pay for this aid, contractor products and services, salaries for all federal workers and members of the military, and the thousands of other federal programs every year. The government pays for everything from the salary of the President, to the rebuilding of Iraq, to basic research conducted at the National Science Foundation, to education grants to fund Head Start programs for pre-school children, to border security, and everything in between. All of these programs and salaries result in the enormous amount of money spent by the federal government. In 2008, federal spending will exceed a staggering $3 trillion.

Figure 4-1 illustrates the annual amounts spent by the U.S. government from 1976 to 2007. Clearly the bar graph shows that there have been steady increases in spending, punctuated by a noticeable increase in spending in recent years. Naturally, because of such things as cost of living increases for salaries and inflation effects on the costs of goods and services, it is not surprising that spending increases year after year.

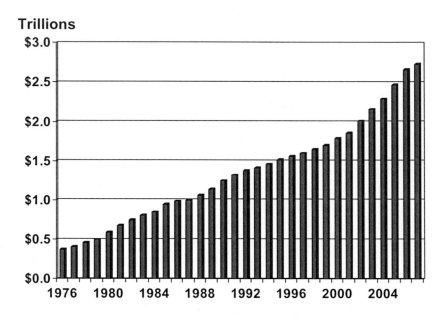

Figure 4-1. Federal Government Spending (1976-2007)[1]

WHERE DOES ALL THE MONEY GO?

The major spending categories for the federal government are shown in Figure 4-2. Defense spending is the single largest category of federal spending. Social Security and Medicare/Medicaid spending closely follow. As the baby

---

[1]   Historical spending figures can be found at the Congressional Budget Office website ("www.cbo.gov"). The spending figures discussed in this book and illustrated in the figures can be found at "http://www.cbo.gov/showdoc.cfm?index=1821&sequence=0".

boomers continue to age and retire, Social Security and Medicare/Medicaid will grow rapidly in coming decades. However, one category of spending that Americans should start to pay attention to is interest on the national debt (discussed in greater detail in Chapter 6). The national debt has exploded in recent years and now stands at over $10.5 trillion. As the historically-low interest rates that we have today rise, and the debt continues to grow, the interest payments required to finance the debt will make up a greater and greater percentage of total federal spending. Unlike other government spending priorities and programs such as defense, Social Security, and Medicare, we get nothing for interest payments. That money just goes to pay creditors for allowing us to borrow money in the past.

Some complain that too much is wasted on unnecessary federal programs. One favorite target for many critics is money sent to foreign countries as part of aid programs. But, the reality is that these programs make up an extremely small amount of total federal budget spending. Not including war costs, which are accounted for in the Department of Defense (DOD) budgets, the total amount of spending on international aid programs in 2007 was $34.7 billion, a large number to be sure, but this amounts to just over one percent of total federal spending in 2007.

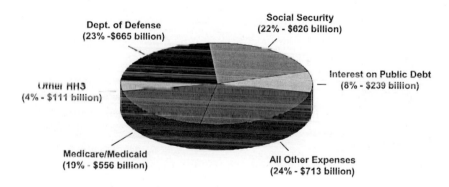

Figure 4-2. Major Categories of Federal Spending (2007)[2]

[2]   Based on the 2007 Treasury Department report entitled, *The Federal Government's Financial Health*. The report is available online at "http://www.gao.gov/financial/citizensguide2008.pdf".

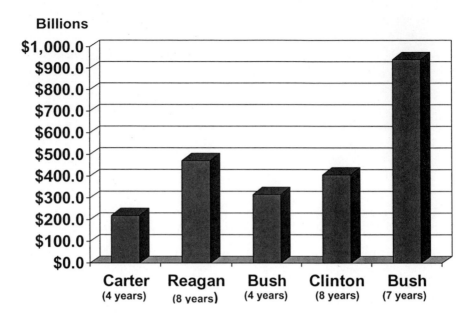

Figure 4-3. Dollar Growth in Annual Government Spending by President[3]

Figure 4-3 shows the dollar increases in the annual amounts spent by the government during the last five presidencies. By the time President Reagan left office, annual spending by the federal government had increased by nearly $500 billion over the amount spent in the final year of the Carter presidency. Over the course of President Clinton's term, total annual spending increased by $400 billion per year. But these increases were modest when compared to the $1 trillion in additional spending that has already been added to annual government budgets under the current President Bush.

In Figure 4-4, we can see the percentage growth in government spending by President. President Reagan's eight years in office ended with an 80 percent increase in annual federal government spending. By comparison, President Clinton's eight years in office ended with federal spending growing by 30 percent – about the same percentage as the growth in spending during the four years of the first President Bush's term.

---

[3] The figures represent the difference between annual government spending in the final year of each President's term and the final year of the prior President's term. For President George W. Bush, the term is through the fourth quarter of 2007.

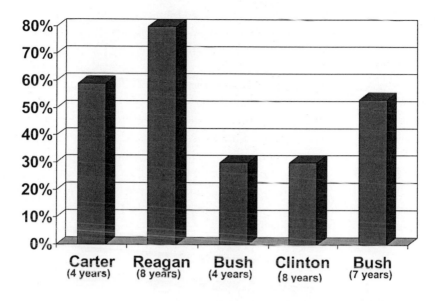

Figure 4-4. Percentage Growth in Annual Government Spending by President[4]

DISCRETIONARY VERSUS PROGRAMMATIC SPENDING

Spending can be divided into two categories – *discretionary spending* and *programmatic spending*. Programmatic spending is spending that is required by law. For example, Social Security beneficiaries receive certain payment amounts that have been established by Congress. As the U.S. population grows, life expectancies extend as a result of drug and medical breakthroughs, and the number of older Americans increases, more money will be required for Social Security beneficiaries; however, the amount paid to each beneficiary remains the same. Congress and the President cannot choose to change the financial benefits for retirees without first passing a new law that legally changes benefit amounts. However, discretionary spending does change from year to year and reflects changing priorities within the government. Presidents can make requests – as President Bush does to fund the war efforts in Iraq and Afghanistan, or to fund cleanup efforts after Hurricane Katrina. Or, Congress can fund new programs. The

---

[4] The figures represent the percentage growth in annual spending over the course of each President's term. For President George W. Bush, the term is through the fourth quarter of 2007. Calculated by taking the difference in spending over the course of each President's term and dividing by the spending at the end of the previous presidency.

system of checks-and-balances requires that both Congress and the President approve new discretionary spending before it can actually be spent. The end result is that programmatic spending increases are "automatic" while discretionary spending amounts change from year to year.

As shown in Figure 4-2, just over 40 percent of federal spending now goes toward paying Social Security and Medicare/Medicaid benefits. Given their rising costs, there are growing concerns about the long-term sustainability of these programs. The fiscal issues surrounding the Social Security program are discussed in Chapter 13, but the next portion of this chapter will focus on the discretionary spending differences between the last several Presidents. By looking at how much growth in discretionary spending occurred under each President (see Figure 4-5), and what the additional discretionary spending was used for, we can learn more about the priorities of each President.

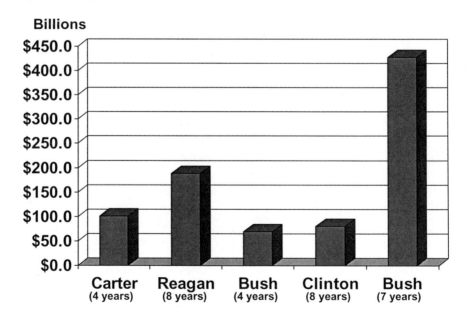

Figure 4-5. Dollar Growth in Annual Discretionary Spending by President[5]

Among the last five Presidents, discretionary spending has increased by the largest dollar amount under George W. Bush. In 2007, the federal government spent more than $400 billion more in annual discretionary spending than when

---

[5] See note 3 in this chapter, except this is for annual discretionary spending rather than total spending.

President Clinton left office in January 2001. When we look at the percentage increases, we can see that there is a major difference in the increases in discretionary spending between the presidencies of George H. W. Bush and Bill Clinton, and the presidencies of Jimmy Carter, Ronald Reagan, and George W. Bush (see Figure 4-6). The latter group saw annual discretionary spending increase by over 50 percent over the course of their presidencies. These increases were far greater than the more modest 15 percent increases during the presidencies of George H. W. Bush and Bill Clinton. It should be noted that the increase in discretionary spending under Jimmy Carter occurred over four years, making it likely that had he served out a second term, he would have overseen the largest percentage increase in discretionary spending among the five Presidents. On the other end of the spectrum, while discretionary spending increased 15 percent during both the first Bush presidency and the Clinton presidency, the Clinton presidency was twice as long. Thus, discretionary spending grew by the slowest pace under President Clinton.

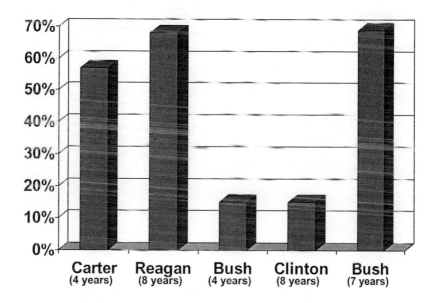

Figure 4-6. Percentage Growth in Annual Discretionary Spending by President[6]

[6] See note 4 in this chapter, except this is for annual discretionary spending rather than total spending.

Not all discretionary spending is the same and there are times when federal spending must increase to cover priorities. For example, during times of war, greater discretionary spending is needed to cover military costs. Figure 4-7 shows defense spending in the final years in office of the past five Presidents. Clearly, we can see the military buildups during the Reagan years and the current Bush presidency.

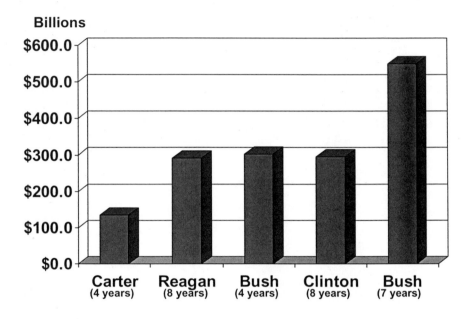

Figure 4-7. Defense Spending by President in Final Year of Term[7]

The percentage changes in defense spending over the course of each President's term in office can be seen in Figure 4-8. Again, we can see that for President Reagan and the current President Bush, defense spending was a major priority. During the Reagan presidency, there was an arms race with the former Soviet Union, and whether one agrees or disagrees with the U.S. policy on Iraq, the fact is that we are there and the military must be funded.

To put the U.S. defense spending into some context, according to CIA estimates, U.S. military spending amounts to about half of all defense spending throughout the world.[8] Even the $300 billion defense budgets under Presidents

---

[7] For the current President Bush , the total defense spending figure for the final year is from 2007.
[8] Data available at the globalsecurity.org website. See
"http://www.globalsecurity.org/military/world/
spending.htm".

Reagan, Bush, and Clinton would amount to one quarter of all military spending in the world today (2008).

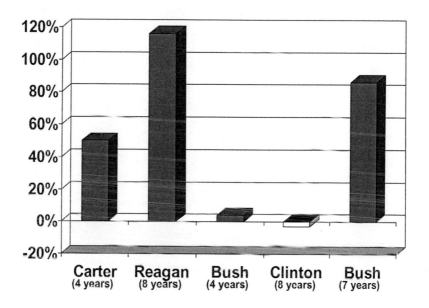

Figure 4-8. Percentage Growth in Annual Defense Spending by President[9]

Non-military domestic discretionary spending is a favorite target of conservatives (again, this does not include programmatic programs such as Social Security and Medicare). These expenditures usually occur as a result of new federal programs that require additional funding. However, as can be seen in Figure 4-9, in terms of dollars, domestic spending has increased during all five of the last presidencies. The increased spending under the current President represents the largest dollar increase. After seven years in office, the government under the leadership of the current President Bush now spends about $150 billion more on an annual basis than it did when President Clinton left office.

---

[9] See note 4 in this chapter, except this is for annual defense spending rather than total spending.

Billions

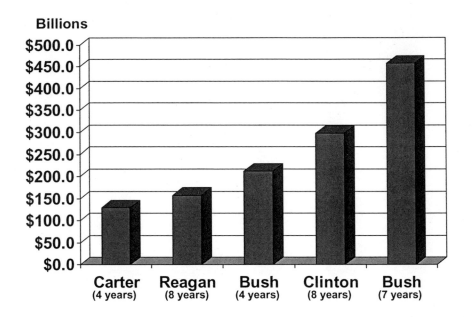

Figure 4-9. Discretionary Domestic Spending by President in Final Year of Term[10]

In terms of percentage increases in discretionary domestic spending, the four years of the Carter Administration resulted in the largest gain (see Figure 4-10). Growth in this spending remained relatively flat over the eight years of the Reagan Administration, but has steadily increased over the course of the last three Presidents. During the eight year term of President Clinton, discretionary domestic spending increased by 41 percent. The first seven years of the current President Bush has seen such spending increase by 53 percent (with one year left in his term). Under the former President Bush, discretionary domestic spending increased by 34 percent, but given that it was over just four years compared to President Clinton's eight years, one can see that this increased spending occurred at a faster pace.

Spending has increased steadily and significantly throughout the terms of the last five Presidents. It is hard to objectively argue that one party or one President has been able to control spending. This fact becomes clear when we look at spending as a percentage of GDP. Table 4-1 provides a summary of the spending figures and the GDP figures for the final year of each presidency (2007 figures are

---

[10] For the current President Bush, the total discretionary domestic spending figure for the final year is from 2007.

shown for President George W. Bush). These figures again allow us to compare across Presidents.

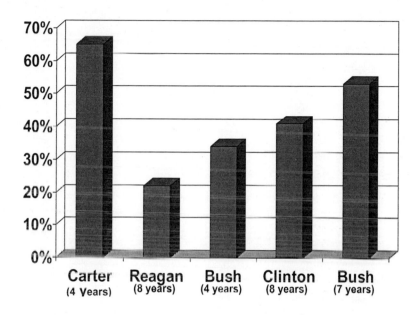

Figure 4-10. Percentage Growth in Annual Discretionary Domestic Spending by President[11]

Table 4-1. Federal Spending and GDP in the Final Year of Each Presidency[12]

President	Spending	GDP	Spending/GDP
Ford	$372 billion	$1.89 trillion	19.7%
Carter	$591 billion	$2.92 trillion	20.2%
Reagan	$1.06 trillion	$5.25 trillion	20.2%
Bush	$1.38 trillion	$6.48 trillion	21.3%
Clinton	$1.79 trillion	$9.95 trillion	18.0%
Bush	$2.73 trillion	$14.07 trillion	19.4%

---

[11] See note 4 in this chapter, except this is for annual discretionary domestic spending rather than total spending.

[12] For the current President Bush, the figures are for the seventh year of his term in office.

There was a bump up in spending relative to GDP with the first President Bush, followed by a significant drop under President Clinton. The trend under the current President is up, with higher spending. What should be clear from the table is that in the final year of President Clinton's term, government spending was at the lowest rate relative to GDP among the five presidencies. The numbers are all fairly close; however, given the enormous size of GDP a one or two percent difference is significant. One percent of a $10 trillion GDP is $100 billion. So had President Clinton's spending amounted to 20 percent of GDP (instead of 18 percent), we would have seen another $200 billion in spending.

Finally, Table 4-2 presents a summary of the growth in annual government spending over the term of each President. For example, under President Carter, the government spent $219 billion more in annual revenues in his last year in office than it did in the last year of the Ford presidency. This represented a 59 percent growth in government spending. As in Chapter 3, Table 4-2 also summarizes the growth in GDP so that one can see how the spending increases compared with the GDP growth over the term of each President.

Table 4-2. Federal Spending and GDP Growth by President[13]

President	Annual Gov't Spending Growth	GDP Growth	% Increase in GDP over Term	% Growth in Annual Gov't Spending over Term
Carter (4 years)	$219 billion	$1.032 trillion	55%	59%
Reagan (8 years)	$474 billion	$2.337 trillion	80%	80%
Bush (4 years)	$317 billion	$1.230 trillion	23%	30%
Clinton (8 years)	$408 billion	$3.470 trillion	54%	30%
Bush (7 years)	$941 billion	$4.120 trillion	41%	53%

As a general rule, growth in spending should not outpace GDP growth. Ideally, the nation's economy is growing faster than the government is spending.

---

[13] The figures represent the difference between the figures in the final year of each President's term and the final year of the prior President's term. For President George W. Bush, the term is through 2007.

If this is the case, then more money is being made and kept by individual citizens and the private sector than is being spent and committed by the government. We can see in Table 4-2 that under Presidents Carter and Reagan, spending growth stayed pace with GDP growth. During President Clinton's term, GDP growth was far greater than growth in spending – again, this is desirable. But, during the two Bush presidencies, spending increased significantly faster than GDP growth.

Now that we have looked at government revenues and spending, we can begin to examine how well (or poorly) our government has functioned from a fiscal standpoint under the last five Presidents. In the following chapter, the difference between government revenues and spending is explored further. When the government spends more than it takes in, it is called a budget deficit. On the other hand, when revenues are greater than spending, we have a budget surplus. The actual budget deficits and surpluses for the U.S. government over the last 30 years are shown and discussed in the next chapter.

Chapter 5

FEDERAL BUDGET DEFICITS AND SURPLUSES

The U.S. economy is difficult for most people to fully comprehend. Even highly-regarded economists and non-partisan policy analysts differ on what is best for the economy. However, one thing that most economists agree on is that significant ongoing deficit spending is bad economic policy. The reasons for this are explored in this chapter.

What is deficit spending? Quite simply, when the amount of money the government spends in a given year is more than the amount of money that the government generates in revenues for that year there is a deficit (i.e., the government engages in deficit spending). If the government spends less than it takes in during the year, there is a budget surplus. Unfortunately, since 1950 there have only been nine years when our government has operated with a surplus.[1]

Integrating the spending and revenue figures from the prior two chapters, Figure 5-1 shows the historical budget deficits and surpluses since 1976. Clearly, and unfortunately, Figure 5-1 shows that deficits are normal for the U.S. government. However, it is also clear that fiscal performance, in terms of the federal budget, was best during the Clinton presidency. In fact, every year of President Clinton's term in office saw improved figures for the budget. He inherited a budget deficit of $290 billion in the final year of the first President Bush, and following eight straight years of improvement, left office with a record budget surplus of $236 billion. Thus, the Clinton Administration oversaw an improvement to the annual budget of $526 billion. For this year (2008), President Bush has projected a deficit of 2.9 percent of GDP, which would amount to more

---

[1] Timothy Bitsberger, "Treasury Debt Management" U.S. Department of Treasury (October 2, 2003). The information was accessed at "http://www.ustreas.gov/press/releases/reports/bitsbergerpresentation.pdf" on June 16, 2008.

than $400 billion.[2] Should the actual federal budget figures for the current fiscal year end with a $400 billion deficit as they are currently projected, this would result in a $636 billion deterioration in the budget situation for the U.S. government since President George W. Bush took office.

Table 5-1 allows us to compare the relative sizes of the deficits at the end of each president's term in office (and the surplus at the end of President Clinton's term), by calculating the deficit as a percentage of GDP.

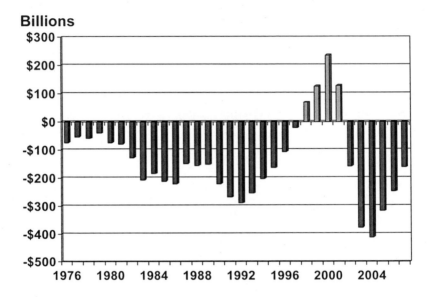

Figure 5-1. Annual Federal Budget Deficits and Surpluses (1976-2007)[3]

Again the figures in Table 5-1 illustrate the significantly better budget situation that President Clinton left at the end of his term. During his eight-year term, the deficit went from 4.5 percent of GDP to a surplus representing 2.4 percent of GDP – by any objective measure that is a remarkable turnaround. One other item that is somewhat surprising is that under President Carter there was significant improvement in the budget over the end of the Ford presidency. Given the memory Americans have of the economic conditions during the Carter Administration, it may also be surprising to realize that the budget situation was better than the budget left by President Reagan. To further illustrate these points

[2] See White House Fact Sheet on the President's Budget (February 4, 2008). Available at "http://www.whitehouse.gov/news/releases/2008/02/20080204.html".
[3] See CBO website at "http://www.cbo.gov/showdoc.cfm?index=1821&sequence=0".

and to compare the budgets between presidents, Table 5-2 provides a summary of the budget changes and GDP growth over the terms of each president.

Table 5-1. Deficits and GDP in the Final Year of Each Presidency[4]

President	Deficit	GDP	Deficit/GDP
Ford	$74 billion	$1.89 trillion	3.9%
Carter	$74 billion	$2.92 trillion	2.5%
Reagan	$155 billion	$5.25 trillion	3.0%
Bush	$290 billion	$6.48 trillion	4.5%
Clinton	($236 billion)*	$9.95 trillion	(2.4%)*
Bush	$162 billion	$14.07 trillion	1.2%

* In 2000 when President Clinton left office there was a $236 billion budget surplus which is why the figures are negative

Table 5-2. Deficit and GDP Growth by President[5]

President	Annual Budget Deficit Growth	GDP Growth	% Increase in GDP over Term	% Increase in Annual Budget Deficit over Term
Carter (4 years)	$100 million	$1.032 trillion	55%	0.1%
Reagan (8 years)	$81 billion	$2.337 trillion	80%	110.3%
Bush (4 years)	$135 billion	$1.230 trillion	23%	87.0%
Clinton (8 years)	($526 billion)*	$3.470 trillion	54%	(181.4%)*
Bush (7 years)	$398 billion	$4.120 trillion	41%	168.6%

* In 2000 when President Clinton left office there was a $236 billion budget surplus which is why the figures are negative (i.e., they represent reductions in deficits that resulted in the surpluses)

---

[4] For the current President Bush, the term is only through his first seven years in office.

[5] The figures represent the difference between the figures in the final year of each President's term and the final year of the prior President's term. For President George W. Bush, the term is through 2007.

Ideally, GDP growth should be faster than growth in budget deficits. From Table 5-2, we can see that this occurred only during the Carter and Clinton Administrations. By contrast, the current President Bush took over an economy that had been booming throughout the 1990s and has overseen another turnaround in the budget that is as bad as Clinton's turnaround was good. GDP growth was strong under President Clinton, and the economy had produced significant government revenues. Spending grew slower than both GDP and government revenues, so it would appear that spending was under control. The end result was a record budget surplus.

Some argue that the economy was slowing when President Clinton's term ended. This is true; however, the economy was still growing at a solid pace. The fact is that GDP grew by 6.3 percent in 1999, 4.6 percent in 2000, 2.7 percent in 2001, and 3.6 percent in 2002, so it is difficult to see how one can argue that the economy was in trouble – even with the 9/11 attacks on the nation. Yet, the U.S. has returned to the several hundred billion dollar deficits that were common throughout the 1980s and early 1990s. This should be a concern for all Americans.

There are fairly obvious reasons for the budget deterioration under President George W. Bush. The 9/11 attacks and Hurricane Katrina did have a significant negative economic impact on the nation, but realistically, we have to expect that hurricanes and disasters will occur – they are nothing new (although the scope and magnitude of the 9/11 attacks were grotesquely unique). If you look back at the Clinton Presidency, we had the first World Trade Center bombing, the Oklahoma City bombing, and Hurricane Andrew. The first President Bush dealt with the Exxon Valdez spill and instability in China with the Tiananmen Square student protests. President Reagan had an escalating arms race with the Soviets, Black Monday's stock market crash, and he was shot. Likewise, President Carter dealt with the oil embargo which caused a major energy crisis, as well as the Iran hostage situation. The point is that things happen during every presidency – we cannot use them as excuses for economic performance.

Beyond the disasters, the real reason budget deficits under President Bush have replaced the surpluses at the end of President Clinton's term can be traced back to the tax cuts combined with record increases in federal spending. The tax cuts slashed government revenues such that the first four years of the Bush Administration (2001-2004) saw government revenues fall below the 2000 revenues in the final year of the Clinton Presidency. Government revenues in 2004 ($1.88 trillion) were 7.2 percent lower than in 2000 ($2.03 trillion). Over that same period, spending increased from $1.79 trillion in 2000, to $2.29 trillion in 2004. This represents a 28 percent increase in spending. Military spending was up 54 percent ($295 billion in 2000 to $454 billion in 2004), and discretionary domestic spending was up 36 percent ($299 billion in 2000 to $408 billion in 2004).

It should not be surprising to anyone that increasing spending by 28 percent at the same time as a 7.2 percent reduction in revenues resulted in large deficits. Just as it would not make sense for a person to immediately go on a dramatic spending spree after he/she took a pay cut, the same rationale should hold for our government – a major cut in revenues should be accompanied by a spending freeze or even spending cuts in order to maintain fiscal responsibility. The result of not holding the line on spending after the tax cuts were implemented led to federal deficits.

To cover the cash shortfalls that result from the annual budget deficits, our government borrows money from private investors, large banks, and foreign central banks (through treasury bills, government bonds, and other securities). The deficit for each year gets added to our national debt. These issues are discussed further in the next chapter.

Chapter 6

U.S. NATIONAL DEBT

There is confusion about the budget deficit and the national debt – they are linked but they are also two very distinct numbers. Budget deficits refer to the annual cash shortfalls that occur year after year (see previous chapter), but the national debt is the total amount the federal government owes. The national debt is the end result of the deficit spending. All of the deficits add up to make up the total national debt.

Many people do not realize that the U.S. has a national debt, and those who do rarely know how large it actually is. Most Americans are probably not concerned about it because it seems abstract and irrelevant to their daily lives. However, it is real money that is owed by our government, and thus, by the American people to various creditors. It has been growing at a rapid pace in recent years, and if this trend does not change, it will become more and more difficult to finance the debt. This is problematic because as the costs to finance the debt increase, there are likely to be significant impacts on future government spending and services.

As of October 23, 2008, the U.S. government owed over $10.5 trillion ($10,524,112,985,802.87 to be more precise[1]), and it is growing by more than $1.5 billion per day.[2] This means that every man, woman, and child living in America is saddled with over $30,000 in government debt. The facts about the debt and complex issues it raises are explored further in this chapter.

---

[1] U.S. National Debt to the penny can be found on the U.S. Treasury Department website at "http://www.treasurydirect.gov/NP/BPDLogin?application=np".

[2] See the U.S. National Debt Clock at "http://www.brillig.com/debt_clock/".

WHO DOES THE GOVERNMENT OWE?

As discussed in the last chapter, in most years, the federal government spends more money than it collects in revenues (deficit spending). Contrary to what many people think, the government cannot just print more money to cover the shortfall and solve the problem. This would negatively impact the value of the dollar and result in inflation (discussed further in Chapter 10). So the government borrows money to pay for the deficit spending. It sounds odd – the government borrowing money – but it is true. There are numerous creditors who hold U.S. federal government debt. These creditors include individual Americans, banks, insurance companies, mutual funds; increasingly, foreign investors and foreign central banks; and even the government itself. Debt held by the government is referred to as *intragovernmental holdings*, and all of the other creditors make up *debt held by the public*.

Intragovernmental holdings currently make up approximately 44 percent of the total national debt ($4.3 trillion).[3] The government borrows money from itself on a regular basis. Sounds confusing and it seems counter-intuitive, but it is really quite simple. The government collects money that is specifically earmarked by law for special programs. Social Security is one such example. According to Congressional Budget Office figures, in 1986, the government collected $16.7 billion more in Social Security taxes than it paid out in Social Security retiree benefits.[4] This grew steadily throughout the latter 1980s and 1990s, and in 1998, the government collected almost $100 billion more in Social Security taxes than it paid out. Last year (2007), the Social Security surplus had grown to $186.5 billion. In total, these hundreds of billions of dollars in excess Social Security taxes have been collected and make up the Social Security Trust fund. According to the annual report prepared by the Social Security Administration, at the end of 2007, the Trust held more than $2 trillion in assets.[5]

However, in reality, the $2 trillion has already been spent by our government – but not on Social Security benefits. Through both Republican and Democratic presidential administrations, as well as when Congress has been controlled by Republicans or by Democrats, the federal government has used the Social Security tax surpluses to pay for annual government programs. Technically, the money has been "borrowed" and has been secured by what amounts to a federal

---

[3] See TreasuryDirect website at "http://www.treasurydirect.gov/NP/BPDLogin?application=np".
[4] See CBO website (www.cbo.gov) at
      "http://www.cbo.gov/showdoc.cfm?index=1821&sequence=0".
[5] Summary of Social Security Administration Trustees' Annual Report. See
      "http://www.ssa.gov/OACT/TRSUM/index.html".

promissory note to pay the borrowed amount back at such time as it is needed. That is, when the annual collected Social Security taxes do not cover the required Social Security benefits payments in a given year, the federal government will be required to begin to pay back the borrowed money. (This and other issues surrounding Social Security are discussed in greater detail in Chapter 13.)

The U.S. Treasury Department refers to the other 56 percent of the total national debt ($6.3 trillion) as "debt held by the public." Essentially, this is the amount that is held by various investors, mutual funds, foreign banks, etc. More specifically, this debt is made up of various short- and long-term U.S. Treasury securities. The U.S. Treasury Department issues out these bills, notes, bonds, and securities with the promise of paying back investors, with interest, at some later date (anywhere from four weeks to 20 years). Traditionally, investors like U.S. Treasury securities because they provide a guaranteed return on money with little risk of losing the invested amount. This is due to the fact that they are backed by the full faith and credit of the U.S. government.

WHY CAN'T THE GOVERNMENT JUST PRINT MORE MONEY AND PAY OFF THE DEBT?

The bottom line is that our government cannot just print more money to pay off the debt because global markets and economies around the world would be thrown into chaos. Most global transactions are pegged to the dollar. That is, foreign currencies are compared to each other relative to the value of a dollar. When goods and services are imported, exported, and otherwise traded across national borders, their relative value is tied to the dollar. Printing another few trillion dollars would destroy the value of the dollar. If the dollar became worthless or lost significant value as a result of newly printed dollars being used to pay off the national debt, the relative values of products and services would become unknown and would need to be re-established. At a minimum, the confusion would have two major immediate negative impacts. First, inflation would explode. As the value of the dollar plunged, firms would simply charge more for their products and services. This would be especially true of imported products. American consumers would be forced to pay rapidly rising prices, but it is unlikely that salaries would rise at the same rate. In recent months, the dollar's value has fallen dramatically, and as a result, we are seeing higher prices for health care, education, clothing, food, gas, etc. Flooding the market with trillions of new dollars would make the current inflationary effects look tame.

The second major effect would be that there would be outrage on the part of foreign banks and governments because they would have to scramble to bring stability to global transactions. There would be no confidence in the value of a dollar and foreign transactions would be pegged to a different currency, such as the Euro or the Japanese yen – which would further boost the value of those currencies relative to the dollar. The resulting loss of confidence in American financial markets would be devastating. Investors would immediately seek shelter in non-American currencies and investments, and those investors who would be willing to invest in American banks would expect very high returns. In other words, we would see much higher interest rates. Obviously, the increased rates would have significant and negative effects on businesses, as they would face higher costs to borrow money for expansion efforts. For individuals, the results would be equally negative as they would face higher credit card rates, car loan rates, and home mortgage rates.

HISTORICAL GROWTH OF THE NATIONAL DEBT

Debt accumulation as a broadly accepted government policy really took hold after President Carter. The national debt grew to over $1 trillion in the early 1980s and has been growing fairly steadily since then. Figure 6-1 shows the growth of the national debt over the last 30 years. There was a period in which debt accumulation slowed considerably in the late 1990s, but since 2001, the growth in the national debt has occurred at a torrid pace.

Figure 6-2 shows the annual figures for national debt as a percentage of GDP from 1976 to 2007. There was a steady increase throughout the 1980s into the mid-1990s. This was followed by a dip and the U.S. is again in a period of rising debt as a percentage of GDP.

Trillions

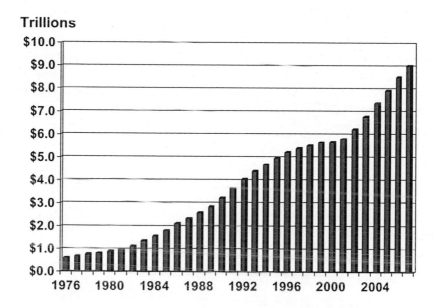

Figure 6-1. Growth of the National Debt (1976-2007)[6]

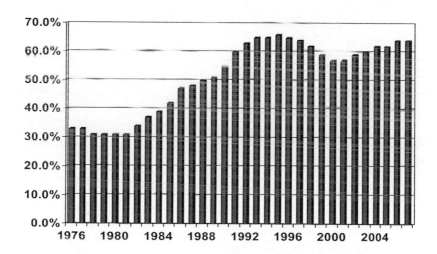

Figure 6-2. National Debt as a Percentage of GDP

---

[6] National debt figures can be found at the U.S. Treasury Department website ("www.treas.gov"). The national debt figures discussed in this book and illustrated in the figures can be found at "http://www.treasurydirect.gov/govt/reports/pd/histdebt/histdebt.htm".

Figure 6-3 segments the debt accumulated during the last five presidential administrations. In terms of total dollars, it is clear that the national debt has increased by the greatest amount under President George W. Bush. During the first seven years of his presidency, the national debt increased by over $3.3 trillion. This is more than the national debt accumulated during the Clinton ($1.6 trillion) and first Bush presidencies ($1.5 trillion) combined.

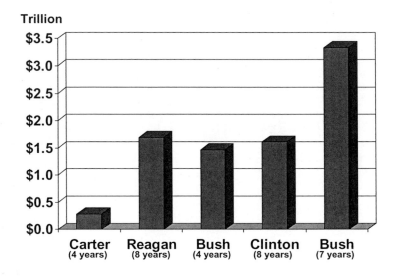

Figure 6-3. National Debt Accumulation by President

Debt in terms of total dollars is not necessarily the best way to compare debt accumulation during the last five presidential administrations. This is due to the fact that a dollar in the 1970s is not the same as a dollar in the 2000s. The country has a far larger economy today than ever before, and as such, more debt can be managed, financed, and absorbed by the economy. For example, a $1 million loan to Bill Gates or Tiger Woods is very different than the same loan to an average American. The reason is obvious – both men have more assets to collateralize the loan, and more capital and income from which to pay back the loan. The same is true for the government. As the U.S. economy grows, there is greater capacity to finance debt, so it is not necessarily surprising that debt increased by the largest dollar figure under the current president because the economy is larger than ever. Thus, in order to better compare debt accumulation during the last five presidencies, we need to look at the percentage increases of debt and the debt as a percentage of GDP.

Figure 6-4 summarizes the percentage growth rate of the national debt during the last five presidencies. At one end of the spectrum, we can see that during the Reagan years, the national debt exploded by 187 percent. At the other end, it grew by 40 percent under President Clinton. In fact, because GDP grew much faster than the national debt during President Clinton's term, the Clinton presidency was the only in the last 30 years in which Americans saw the debt as a percentage of GDP drop significantly.

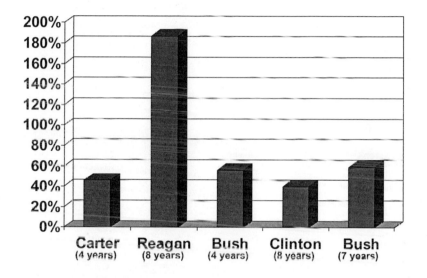

Figure 6-4. Percentage Growth of National Debt by President

Dividing the national debt by the GDP yields a good indicator of how manageable the national debt is. Figure 6-5 shows that at the end of the Carter presidency, the national debt stood at about 30 percent of GDP. By the end of the Reagan presidency, the national debt had grown to half of GDP. It grew further under the first President Bush, shrunk under President Clinton, and has again risen under President George W. Bush.

Economists can quibble about what a "reasonable" or even "desirable" debt load may be, and when an economy is carrying too much debt. However, most would agree that reducing overall debt, or at least reducing it as a percentage of GDP are desirable goals. That is why it is useful to pay attention to trends over time. Toward this end, Figure 6-6 illustrates the changes in the debt as a percentage of GDP over the terms of each of last five presidents.

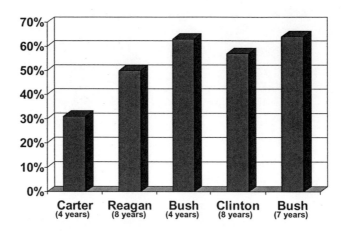

Figure 6-5. National Debt as a Percentage of GDP by President

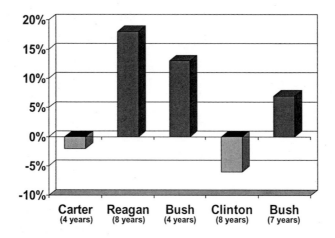

Figure 6-6. Change of National Debt as a Percentage of GDP by President

Presidents Carter and Clinton left office with debt as a percentage of GDP having been reduced from the time they took office. For Presidents Reagan, George H.W. Bush, and George W. Bush, the national debt grew faster than GDP which is why they left office (or will likely leave office, in the case of the current President Bush) with debt as a percentage of GDP having gone up.

To close out the chapter, Table 6-1 summarizes the national debt and GDP numbers at the end of each president's term. What jumps out is the growth in the national debt as a percentage of GDP over the last 30 years. More specifically, the

12 years of the Reagan and Bush presidencies saw the figure double. Consistent with Figures 6-2, 6-5 and 6-6, debt as a percentage of GDP eased back at the end of the Clinton presidency, but it has risen dramatically under the current President Bush.

Table 6-1. National Debt and GDP in Final Year of each Presidency[7]

President	National Debt	GDP	Debt/GDP
Ford	$620 billion	$1.89 trillion	32.8%
Carter	$908 billion	$2.92 trillion	31.1%
Reagan	$2.60 trillion	$5.25 trillion	49.5%
Bush	$4.06 trillion	$6.48 trillion	62.7%
Clinton	$5.67 trillion	$9.95 trillion	57.0%
Bush	$9.01 trillion	$14.07 trillion	64.0%

The actual GDP growth and debt accumulation figures in total dollars are shown in Table 6-2. What should be obvious is that better fiscal performance is indicated by debt growing at a slower pace than GDP growth. As shown in Figure 6-6 and the financial figures in Table 6-2, this was accomplished only during the Carter and Clinton Administrations.

Table 6-2. National Debt and GDP Growth by President[8]

President	National Debt Growth	GDP Growth	% Increase in GDP over Term	% Increase in Nat Debt over Term
Carter (4 years)	$0.287 trillion	$1.032 trillion	55%	46%
Reagan (8 years)	$1.695 trillion	$2.337 trillion	80%	187%
Bush (4 years)	$1.462 trillion	$1.230 trillion	23%	56%
Clinton (8 years)	$1.610 trillion	$3.470 trillion	54%	40%
Bush (7 years)	$3.664 trillion	$4.120 trillion	41%	65%

---

[7] For the current President Bush, the figures are for the seventh year of his term in office.

[8] The figures represent the difference between the figures in the final year of each President's term and the final year of the prior President's term. For President George W. Bush, the term is through 2007.

Chapter 7

U.S. NATIONAL DEBT HELD BY FOREIGNERS

This chapter builds on the discussion and figures in the previous chapter. In addition to the explosion in debt over the last 30 years, there is an even more alarming trend – the willingness on the part of the federal government to borrow enormous sums of money from foreign investors. The national debt is a growing problem, but the rapid rise in debt owed to foreigners threatens the very sovereignty of the United States.

As discussed in the previous chapter, much of the money the U.S. government raises to finance the national debt and pay for the deficit spending is raised through the sale of U.S. Treasury securities (i.e., government bonds and government notes). However, the massive accumulation of national debt and the record deficits we have seen in recent years requires the government to borrow heavily from foreign governments and foreign central banks through the sale of Treasury securities to the public. Quite simply, there are not enough investors or U.S. banks who are willing and/or able to fund our nation's debt and deficits.

As of August 2008, foreigners held over $2.7 trillion in U.S. government debt (i.e. U.S. Treasury securities).[1] Consider what this really means – Americans owe $2.7 trillion to foreign governments, foreign sovereign wealth funds (i.e., mutual funds and investment funds owned by foreign governments), and foreign central banks. While still not necessarily in our nation's best interest, it might not be so bad if all of our debt was held by our friends and allies in the world – but this is simply not the case. We owe China $541 billion and Russia $74.4 billion. We are not allies with these countries, and often oppose each other on various geo-political matters. We owe nearly $180 billion to OPEC nations which include openly-hostile nations to the U.S. Mexico and Carribean banking centers hold

---

[1] The U.S. Treasury Department provides a summary of the *Major Foreign Holders of U.S. Debt* that is updated monthly. Available online at "http://www.treas.gov/tic/mfh.txt".

over $180 billion in U.S. debt. While the latter group is more friendly toward us, the debt they now hold makes it more difficult for the U.S. to demand assistance with problems such as illegal immigration or drug trafficking should they choose not to cooperate.

Figure 7-1 illustrates the growth in the U.S. debt held by foreigners from 1976 to 2007. As can be seen in the figure, there have been two periods of dramatic growth – the mid-1990s and from 2001 to the present.

Trillions

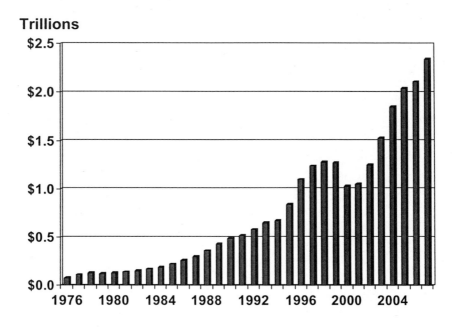

Figure 7-1. Debt Held by Foreigners (1976-2007)[2]

The overall size of the debt held by foreigners is enormous, but the rapid increase – especially since 2000 – is truly breathtaking. At the end of 2000, China, Hong Kong, and Taiwan combined held less than $135 billion in U.S. Treasury Securities and OPEC (which includes Iran) held less than $50 billion. Today, China, Hong Kong, and Taiwan combined now hold over $600 billion and OPEC now holds over $150 billion of our debt. Russia held no U.S. debt just two years ago. But, the Russian government has steadily been buying up U.S. Treasury securities and it now holds $60 billion of the U.S. national debt. These shifts in

[2]   Based on U.S. Treasury Department figures available on the St. Louis Federal Reserve Bank website at "http://research.stlouisfed.org/fred2/data/FDHBFIN.txt".

the balance of economic power are happening so rapidly that most Americans probably are completely unaware that such shifts are taking place.

The debt accumulation figures are just as bad – if not worse – when they are considered with respect to U.S. GDP (see Figure 7-2). At the end of the 1970s, foreign-held debt was about four percent of GDP. By the end of the 1980s, it had more than doubled to nearly nine percent of GDP. Following President Clinton's term in 2000, it had again ticked up to about 10 percent of GDP. However, at the end of 2007, the figure had jumped to over 16 percent of GDP and there is no real end in sight because the economy has weakened in recent years. With tax revenues shrinking but spending continuing to rise, the dependence on foreign cash to cover the growing budget deficits is increasing.

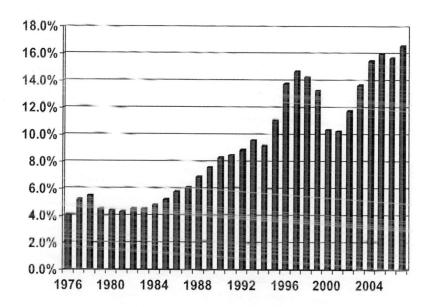

Figure 7-2. Debt Held by Foreigners as a Percentage of GDP (1976-2007)

The greatest increase in the debt held by foreigners has come under the current President Bush (see Figure 7-3). In 2000, when he took office foreigners held about $1 trillion in U.S. government debt. Seven a half years later, the foreign-held debt has ballooned to $2.6 trillion. In fact, the accumulation of foreign-held debt under the President George W. Bush has dwarfed the total accumulation of such debt under all previous presidents combined.

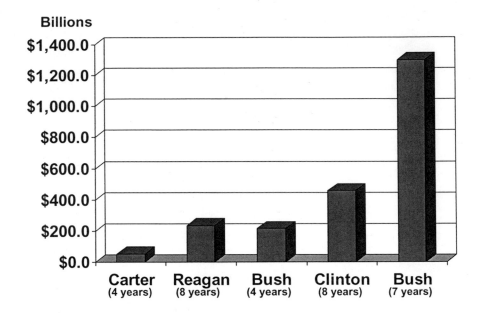

Figure 7-3. Dollar Increase in the Debt Held by Foreigners by President

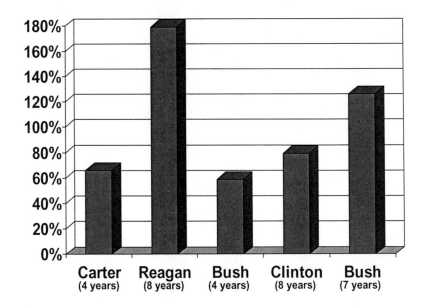

Figure 7-4. Percentage Growth in the Debt Held by Foreigners by President

The percentage growth of debt held by foreigners under each President is slightly more favorable for the current President Bush (see Figure 7-4). It shows that this debt accumulation increased by a far greater percentage during the Reagan presidency. However, it should be noted that the data only includes the first seven years of President George W. Bush's term. If one includes the accumulation of this debt in 2008, the percentage rises significantly for President Bush. In fact, it has increased by more than 30 percent through May 2008. At the current pace of accumulation, by the time President Bush leaves office, he may very well overtake President Reagan's dubious position as having had the greatest percentage growth in foreign-held debt among the last five U.S. Presidents.

Finally, Table 7-1 summarizes the total debt held by foreigners and GDP at the end of each president's term. Comparing the figures for the last five presidencies, it is apparent that foreign debt as a percentage of GDP has risen steadily over the last 30 years. However, by far, the percentage increased by the greatest amount under President George W. Bush.

Table 7-1. Foreign-Held Debt and GDP in the Final Year of Each Presidency[3]

President	Foreign-Held Debt	GDP	Foreign-Held Debt/GDP
Ford	$78 billion	$1.89 trillion	4.1%
Carter	$130 billion	$2.92 trillion	4.5%
Reagan	$362 billion	$5.25 trillion	6.9%
Bush	$577 billion	$6.48 trillion	8.9%
Clinton	$1.0 trillion	$9.95 trillion	10.1%
Bush	$2.3 trillion	$14.07 trillion	16.3%

In an effort to better analyze the fiscal performance of the government, with respect to accumulation of foreign-held debt during each president's term in office, the growth percentages for GDP and the debt held by foreigners are shown in Table 7-2. Common sense would suggest that better fiscal performance is realized when foreign-held debt does not grow as fast as GDP. However, as shown in Table 7-2, this has not happened during the terms of any of the last five Presidents.

---

[3] For the current President Bush, the figures are for the seventh year of his term in office.

Table 7-2. Foreign-Held Debt and GDP Growth by President[4]

President	Foreign-Held Debt Growth	GDP Growth	% Increase in GDP over Term	% Inc. in Foreign-Held Debt over Term
Carter (4 years)	$52 billion	$1.032 trillion	55%	66%
Reagan (8 years)	$233 billion	$2.337 trillion	80%	179%
Bush (4 years)	$215 billion	$1.230 trillion	23%	59%
Clinton (8 years)	$458 billion	$3.470 trillion	54%	79%
Bush (7 years)	$1.3 trillion	$4.120 trillion	41%	126%

---

[4] The figures represent the difference between the figures in the final year of each President's term and the final year of the prior President's term. For President George W. Bush, the term is through 2007.

Chapter 8

U.S. CURRENT ACCOUNT

Every year, the U.S. exports finished goods and services and imports finished goods and services. When the nation imports more than it exports there is a trade deficit. When exports exceed imports, the U.S. enjoys a trade surplus. As a general rule, it is better to export more than the country imports. When this happens, the country is drawing in more capital and accumulating wealth from outside countries. If, on the other hand, the country imports more than it exports, there is a net flow of U.S. wealth out of the nation and to other countries that the U.S. has a trade deficit with.

The federal government tracks what is known as the *current account* for the nation.[1] The current account is essentially a measure of the net flow of dollars in and out of the country. It is primarily made up of our trade balance (trade exports minus trade imports), but also includes such things as interest earned on foreign investments less interest paid out on U.S. debt held by foreigners as well as foreign aid (also subtracted from the current account). Just as with the trade of goods and services described above, when the current account is positive, the country enjoys a current account surplus. When it is negative, the U.S. has a current account deficit. At a minimum, the U.S. should remain neutral with respect to the current account. However, a measure of a nation's economic power and financial strength is a positive current account (i.e., a surplus). Essentially, this means that products and services from within national borders are desired by customers around the world, and it also means that little debt is owed to foreign entities.

---

[1] Current account figures can be found at the U.S. Bureau of Economic Analysis website ("www.bea.gov"). The current account figures discussed in this book and illustrated in the figures can be found at "http://www.bea.gov/international/bp_web/simple.cfm?anon=71 &table_id=1&area_id=3".

Unfortunately, there has been a remarkable downward shift in our nation's net current account position over the last three decades. Figure 8-1 shows the U.S. current account from 1976 to 2007. What is clear from this figure is that there has been a rapid deterioration in the current account, and the nation now has a net outflow of dollars and U.S. wealth to the tune of about $750 billion per year. Over the long-term, this is unsustainable. It poses a serious threat to our economic strength both domestically and around the world.

As a percentage of GDP, the current account deficit has steadily increased to over five percent of GDP (see Figure 8-2). Unfortunately, with the nation's rapid increase in debt held by the public and the debt owed to foreigners (discussed in the last two chapters) it is likely that U.S. government interest payments on that national debt will continue to rise. In addition, over the first half of 2008, oil prices increased by about 50 percent. Given our significant oil imports, this will further tilt the trade imbalance in favor of foreign oil producers. The rising national debt and high oil prices are not likely to change over the next few years. If there are no significant improvements for the U.S. on these two factors, the U.S. current account balance will not improve and will likely continue to erode.

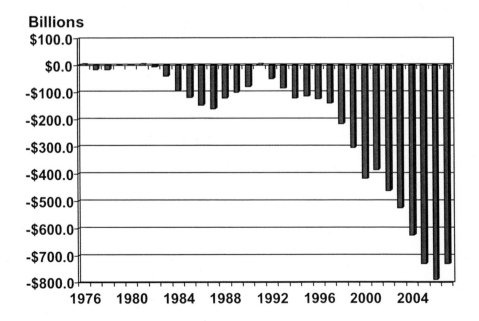

Figure 8-1. U.S. Current Account (1976-2007)

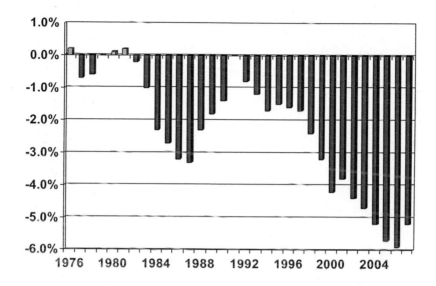

Figure 8-2. U.S. Current Account as a Percentage of GDP (1976-2007)

Up until the early 1980s, the U.S. had no significant imbalance with foreign countries. The nation largely enjoyed a neutral and often small current account surplus from year to year. However, this all changed under President Reagan. It worsened by the end of President Clinton's term, and it has continued to worsen under President George W. Bush (see Figure 8-3).

Figure 8-4 illustrates the percentage changes in the current account over the course of the last five presidencies. While the last two presidents saw the largest declines in the current account in terms of absolute dollars, there is no question that the largest percentage shift in the current account occurred during the Reagan Administration. During those eight years, the U.S. current account deficit grew by more than 5000 percent. This figure dwarfs the declines during the other four presidencies.

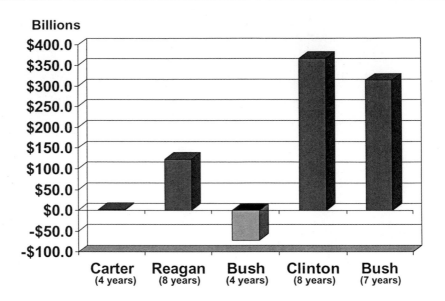

Figure 8-3. U.S. Current Account Changes by President[2]

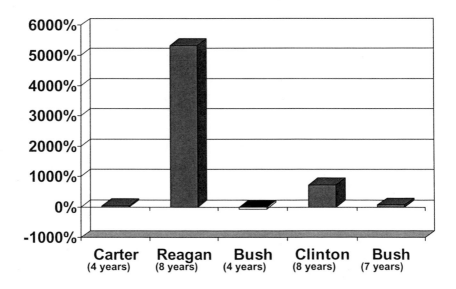

Figure 8-4. Percentage Change in U.S. Current Account Deficit by President

---

[2] The figures represent the difference between the figures in the final year of each President's term and the final year of the prior President's term. For President George W. Bush, the term is through 2007.

Changes in the current account relative to changes in the GDP are provided in the final two tables of this chapter. Table 8-1 summarizes the current account and GDP at the end of each president's term. Comparing the figures for the last five presidencies, and as shown in the earlier figures, one can see that there has been significant erosion in the U.S. current account. The erosion has occurred at a far faster pace than growth in GDP over the same period in time. The largest negative shift, in terms of dollars, occurred over the eight-year term of the Clinton presidency. During those years, the current account as a percentage of GDP fell from a deficit that was less than one percent of GDP to a deficit that was over four percent of GDP.

Table 8-1. U.S. Current Account and GDP
in the Final Year of Each Presidency[3]

President	Current Account	GDP	CA/GDP
Ford	$4.3 billion	$1.89 trillion	0.2%
Carter	$2.3 billion	$2.92 trillion	0.1%
Reagan	($121.2 billion)	$5.25 trillion	(2.3%)
Bush	($50.1 billion)	$6.48 trillion	(0.8%)
Clinton	($417.4 billion)	$9.95 trillion	(4.2%)
Bush	($731.2 billion)	$14.07 trillion	(5.2%)

Among the last five presidents, the current account improved only under the first President Bush (see Table 8-2). Under President Carter, the current account worsened by 46 percent. However, the U.S. still maintained a surplus and GDP improved by a faster rate than the decline (55 percent). This would suggest that during the Carter presidency the net change in the current account was manageable. For the other three presidents the worsening current accounts grew by a greater percentage than the percentage gains in the GDP, which can only be interpreted as negative performance with respect to current account.

---

[3] For the current President Bush, the figures are for the seventh year of his term in office.

Table 8-2. U.S. Current Account Changes and GDP Growth by President[4]

President	CA Change	GDP Growth	% Increase in GDP over Term	% Change in CA over Term
Carter (4 years)	($1.2 billion)	$1.032 trillion	55%	(46%)
Reagan (8 years)	($123.5 billion)	$2.337 trillion	80%	(5329%)
Bush (4 years)	$71.5 billion	$1.230 trillion	23%	59%
Clinton (8 years)	($367.3 billion)	$3.470 trillion	54%	(734%)
Bush (7 years)	($313.8 billion)	$4.120 trillion	41%	(75%)

---

[4] The figures represent the difference between the figures in the final year of each President's term and the final year of the prior President's term. For President George W. Bush, the term is through 2007.

Chapter 9

U.S. UNEMPLOYMENT RATE

High unemployment is obviously a negative economic sign for a nation. However, at the other end of the spectrum, a country that has no unemployment is at risk of inflationary pressure that can also be a real negative for the country. If the labor market is overly tight, employers are forced to respond with rising wages and other incentives (e.g., extended vacations, signing bonuses, superior health benefits) in order to attract the best employees. This can trigger rising prices on goods and services as firms pass on the increased labor costs to clients and customers. In addition, tight labor markets force employers to look for labor outside of the domestic market. Zero unemployment would result in jobs shifting to other labor markets around the world.

Figure 9-1 shows the U.S. unemployment rate at the end of each year from 1976 to 2007. Clearly, there is a cyclical nature to the unemployment pattern as the rate fluctuates over time.

Figure 9-2 shows the change in the unemployment rate from the beginning to the end of each of the last five presidencies. Unemployment fell over the full terms of the Carter, Reagan, and Clinton Administrations. The rate increased under the first President Bush and is rising under the current President Bush. However, by looking at the yearly figures (see Figure 9-1), we can see a more complete story emerge. For example, in the final year of President Carter's term, unemployment rose from under six percent in 1979 to over seven percent in 1980. This likely caused great angst among the voters who soured on President Carter.

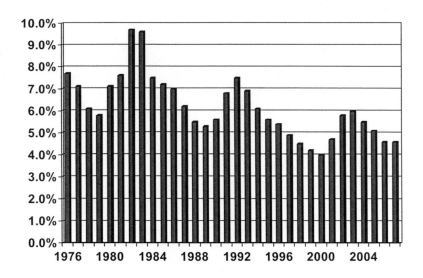

Figure 9-1. U.S. Unemployment Rate (1976-2007)[1]

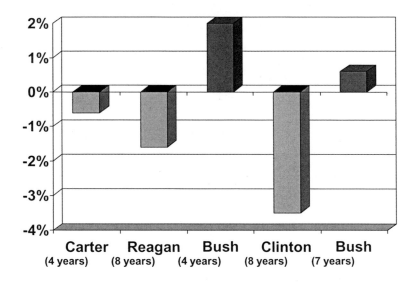

Figure 9-2. U.S. Unemployment Rate Changes by President

---

[1]   Unemployment figures can be found at the U.S. Bureau of Labor Statistics website ("www.bls.gov"). The unemployment figures discussed in this book and illustrated in the figures can be found at "ftp://ftp.bls.gov/pub/special.requests/lf/aat1.txt".

The rising unemployment rates in 1980 and 1992 likely contributed to the re-election campaign losses suffered by President Carter and President George H.W. Bush. Following a peak unemployment rate in the early 1980s, there was a steady decrease in unemployment. This was also true throughout the Clinton presidency. Just as Presidents Carter and the first President Bush were probably stung by rising unemployment, the falling unemployment rates under Presidents Reagan and Clinton likely helped them remain popular with the American people. Not only do economic policies have impacts on the nation, but they can directly affect a President's approval ratings. The importance of timing should not be overlooked. Had unemployment not shot up in the final years of the Carter and first Bush Administrations, they likely would have been re-elected. On the other hand, their economic policies contributed to the rising unemployment rates, so one should not simply attribute rising or falling unemployment to bad or good luck.

Table 9-1 shows the unemployment rates and GDP at the end of each president's term. Again, while GDP increased during the presidential terms' of each man, there were big differences in the unemployment rates. The far right column shows that during the full terms of the Carter, Reagan, and Clinton Administrations, the unemployment rate dropped by eight percent, 23 percent, and 47 percent, respectively. Both Presidents Bush saw significant increases in unemployment during their terms.

Table 9-1. U.S. Unemployment Rate Changes and GDP Growth by President[2]

President	Unemployment Rate at End of Term	GDP Growth	% Increase in GDP over Term	% Change in Unemployment Rate over Term
Carter (4 years)	7.1%	$1.032 trillion	55%	(8%)
Reagan (8 years)	5.5%	$2.337 trillion	80%	(23%)
Bush (4 years)	7.5%	$1.230 trillion	23%	36%
Clinton (8 years)	4.0%	$3.470 trillion	54%	(47%)
Bush (7 years)	4.6%	$4.120 trillion	41%	15%

---

[2] The figures represent the difference between the figures in the final year of each President's term and the final year of the prior President's term. For President George W. Bush, the term is through 2007.

Chapter 10

U.S. INFLATION RATE

Inflation is a relatively easy concept to understand, but many people do not understand what it is, or the implications of high versus low inflation. Inflation is related to the constant rise in prices and costs for goods and services in an economy. A gallon of milk today costs more than it did 20 years ago, and will likely cost even more in 20 years. The reason is because inflation makes the value of the dollar go down over time. There are more dollars in circulation and costs tend to rise over time.

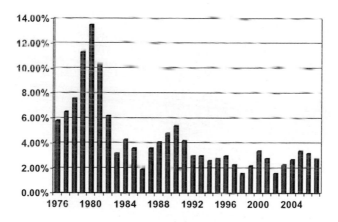

Figure 10-1. U.S. Inflation Rate (1976-2007)[1]

---

[1] U.S. inflation figures can be found at the U.S. Bureau of Labor Statistics website ("www.bls.gov"). The inflation figures discussed in this book and illustrated in the figures can be found at "ftp://ftp.bls.gov/pub/special.requests/cpi/cpiai.txt".

The U.S. inflation rate is measured by the Consumer Price Index (CPI), and many of the U.S. government's economic and monetary policies are geared toward maintaining an annual CPI increase of about two to three percent. When the CPI grows by more than three percent, the Federal Reserve Board (Fed) takes action to adjust monetary policies. For example, the Fed may raise interest rates to encourage savings and cut down spending in an effort to cut dollar liquidity in the market. This puts fewer dollars in circulation which tends to increase the value of the dollar (fewer dollars are available to purchase goods and services).

Figure 10-1 shows the annual CPI figures from 1976 to 2007. The numbers represent the percentage change in the CPI from the previous year. While there is some fluctuation from year to year, inflation has been relatively tame since the early 1990s. That is, the annual CPI figures have not gone above four percent since then. Looking further back, inflation has been largely under control since the early 1980s. Prior to then, the country experienced the pain of double digit inflation for several years.

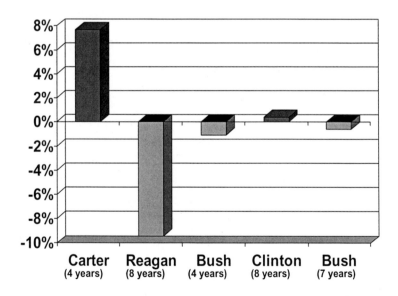

Figure 10-2. U.S. Inflation Rate Changes by President[2]

---

[2] The figures represent the difference between the figures in the final year of each President's term and the final year of the prior President's term. For President George W. Bush, the term is through 2007.

Figure 10-2 shows the percentage changes in the inflation rate during the full terms of the last five presidents. For both Presidents Bush and President Clinton, inflation has not really changed. There was a big jump in inflation under President Carter, followed by an even larger drop in the inflation rate under President Reagan. This likely played a major part in the failure of President Carter to win re-election to a second term, as well as contributing to the fond memories many have about President Reagan and his term in office.

Table 10-1 provides a summary of the inflation and GDP growth rates at the end of each president's term. Ideally, one would want to see little to no inflation growth (or even a reduction in the inflation rate), combined with significant GDP growth. This has been the case for four of the last five Presidents. Only President Carter held office during a significant rise in inflation. Making matters worse for him, there was a large increase in inflation between his third year and his fourth year in office, which all but doomed his reelection bid.

Table 10-1. U.S. Inflation Rate Changes and GDP Growth by President[3]

President	Inflation Rate at End of Term	GDP Growth	% Increase in GDP over Term	% Change in Inflation Rate over Term
Carter (4 years)	13.5%	$1.032 trillion	55%	133%
Reagan (8 years)	4.1%	$2.337 trillion	80%	(70%)
Bush (4 years)	3.0%	$1.230 trillion	23%	(27%)
Clinton (8 years)	3.4%	$3.470 trillion	54%	13%
Bush (7 years)	2.8%	$4.120 trillion	41%	(18%)

---

[3] The figures represent the difference between the figures in the final year of each President's term and the final year of the prior President's term. For President George W. Bush, the term is through 2007.

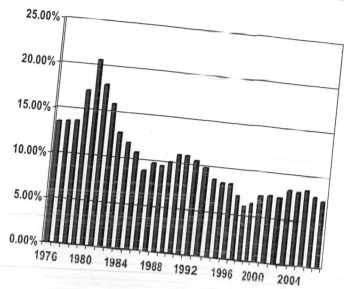

Figure 11-1. U.S. Misery Index (1976-2007)[1]

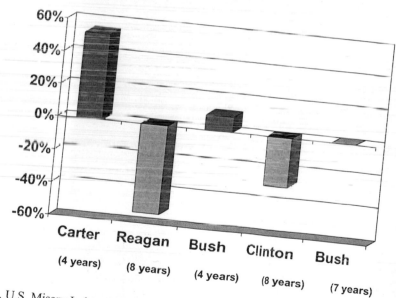

| Carter | Reagan | Bush | Clinton | Bush |
| (4 years) | (8 years) | (4 years) | (8 years) | (7 years) |

Figure 11-2. U.S. Misery Index Changes by President

The figures and graphics in this chapter are based on adding the figures used in Chapters 9 and 10.

Chapter 11

U.S. MISERY INDEX

An unofficial measure of the health of the U.S. economy is what is known as the *misery index*. The index is simply the sum of the unemployment rate and the rate of inflation. Obviously, as it increases the misery of the average American goes up.

Using the data presented in the two previous chapters, the misery index can be calculated for the nation. Figure 11-1 illustrates the misery index over the last 30 years. We can see that following the 1980 peak of 20.7 percent there was a steady decline in the misery index for six years. After a modest increase, it again fell through most of the 1990s. For more than a decade, this misery index has remained fairly manageable and has hovered between six and nine percent.

The misery index grew rapidly during the Carter Administration, and declined significantly under Presidents Reagan and Clinton (see Figure 11-2). Again, th changes in the misery index are likely to have contributed to President Carter failed re-election bid. It undoubtedly played a major part in why President Car is not remembered as a strong president. At the other end of the spectrum, falling misery indices over the courses of the Reagan and Clinton presidencies likely to have greatly contributed to the fond memories and enduring populari both men.

Table 11-1 provides a summary of the misery index changes and GDP growth rates at the end of each president's term. For President Carter, all of the gain in GDP was offset by an equally significant gain in the misery index. For President Reagan, and to a lesser degree President Clinton, the substantial growth in GDP was enhanced by the significant shrinking of the misery index. For both Presidents Bush, the misery index hovered with little to no change, and GDP growth was more moderate for both men.

Table 11-1. U.S. Misery Index Changes and GDP Growth by President[2]

President	Misery Index at End of Term	GDP Growth	% Increase in GDP over Term	% Change in Misery Index over Term
Carter (4 years)	20.6%	$1.032 trillion	55%	53%
Reagan (8 years)	9.6%	$2.337 trillion	80%	(53%)
Bush (4 years)	10.5%	$1.230 trillion	23%	9%
Clinton (8 years)	7.4%	$3.470 trillion	54%	(30%)
Bush (7 years)	7.4%	$4.120 trillion	41%	0%

---

[2] The figures represent the difference between the figures in the final year of each President's term and the final year of the prior President's term. For President George W. Bush, the term is through 2007.

STRENGTH OF THE U.S. DOLLAR

In many countries around the world, it is relatively common for consumers to purchase goods and services in dollars. The dollar is the world's currency and the fact in that most financial transactions and major commodities trading around the world are done by using the dollar to set prices. When the dollar is strong, goods imported into the U.S. are cheaper because the dollar can purchase more in foreign markets than it can when the dollar is weak. When the dollar falls, imported goods become more expensive and U.S. exports tend to rise because U.S. products become cheaper to foreign customers.

Countries that have stronger currencies have a great advantage in the global marketplace. Firms and investors from such countries are able to buy up foreign assets in markets that have currencies that are devalued against their currency. Thus, when the U.S. dollar is strong, American corporations can span the globe and buy up foreign firms/assets, but when the dollar falls, it is the foreign firms that have the advantage. When the dollar falls, foreign firms buy up U.S. firms/assets at a cheaper price. For all of the above reasons, there is great interest, both in the U.S. and around the world, in the value of the dollar.

There are a number of ways to track the value of the U.S. dollar. One can find actual exchange rates and trade currencies on foreign exchange (forex) markets for individual currencies around the world. For example, on any given day, up-to-the-minute exchange rates are readily available and one can convert dollars into euros, Chinese yuan, British pounds, Japanese yen, Indian rupees, Russian rubles, or whatever currency one may be interested in. However, while the individual currency exchange rates may be important for tourists who plan to visit individual countries, country-by-country exchange rates do not give an overall sense of how the dollar is faring across the globe. Consider that the Indian economy may be growing and the rupee may gain against the dollar, but at the same time it could be possible for the Japanese yen to fall against the dollar.

To address the issue of how to better value the dollar relative to the world economy, there are indices that consider the dollar's strength against a basket of foreign currencies. These indices use weighting schemes to give certain currencies – such as the euro or the Japanese yen – more weight than other nation's currencies. The basic idea of such an index is to provide those who are interested in the broader value of the dollar (i.e., currency traders, Wall Street analysts, policy makers) with an easy way to see the global value of the dollar. One example of such an index is the U.S. Dollar Index on the N.Y. Board of Trade (ticker symbol DX-Y.NYB). Currency traders and investors can see the value of the dollar and publicly trade futures on the dollar.

The purpose of this chapter is to focus on the macro-level changes in the value of the dollar over time. To do that, this chapter illustrates the changing value of the dollar based on the Federal Reserve Bank of Atlanta's trade-weighted dollar index.[1] It has been used to track the value of the U.S. dollar against foreign currencies for several decades. Figure 12-1 illustrates the changing value of the dollar index from 1976 to 2007. The figure clearly shows that the dollar has gone through cyclical changes with two peaks in value over the last 3 decades. Just to be clear, there is a very high correlation with the figures in the U.S. Dollar Index described in the previous paragraph and you would find exactly the same trend.

---

[1] For more information on the index, visit the Federal Reserve Bank of Atlanta website and read the
    1999 Economic Review article on the subject at
    "http://www.frbatlanta.org/filelegacydocs/acree.pdf".

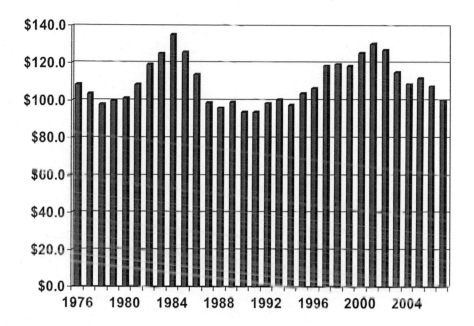

Figure 12-1. U.S. Dollar Index (1976-2007)[2]

In terms of absolute dollar value changes, Figure 12-2 shows that the dollar gained considerably over President Clinton's term in office and has since declined dramatically. Figure 12-3 illustrates the percentage changes over the course of each president's full term in office. Again, we can see that the Clinton Administration enjoyed the greatest percentage increase in the value of the dollar.

To compare the performance of the dollar across the presidential terms, Table 12-1 is offered. It shows GDP growth and the changing value of the Atlanta Fed's dollar index over the terms of each of the last five presidents. The best case scenario is when GDP growth is high and the dollar strength improves dramatically. This only occurred during the Clinton presidency.

---

[2] Data available at the Federal Reserve Bank of Atlanta website at "http://www.frbatlanta.org
/DollarIndex/user/dsp_indexes.cfm".

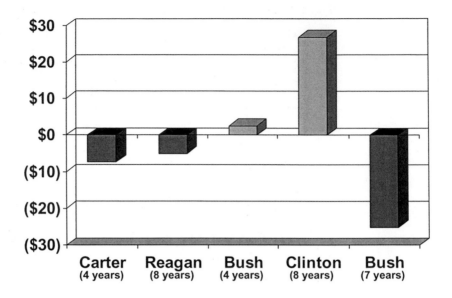

Figure 12-2. U.S. Dollar Index Changes by President

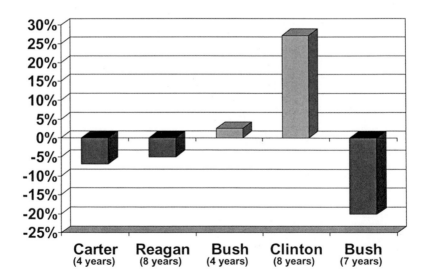

Figure 12-3. Percentage Change in U.S. Dollar Index by President

Table 12-1. U.S. Dollar Index Changes and GDP Growth by President[3]

President	Dollar Index Change	GDP Growth	% Increase in GDP over Term	% Change in Dollar Index over Term
Carter (4 years)	($7.36)	$1.032 trillion	55%	(7%)
Reagan (8 years)	($5.04)	$2.337 trillion	80%	(5%)
Bush (4 years)	$2.43	$1.230 trillion	23%	3%
Clinton (8 years)	$26.84	$3.470 trillion	54%	27%
Bush (7 years)	($25.15)	$4.120 trillion	41%	(20%)

[3] The figures represent the difference between the figures in the final year of each President's term and the final year of the prior President's term. For President George W. Bush, the term is through 2007.

Chapter 13

SOCIAL SECURITY

Social Security is one of the most popular and successful federal programs in the history of the nation. It provides a basic safety net for millions of Americans. Signed into law in 1935, monthly benefits checks were first issued in January 1940.[1] Since that time, Social Security has allowed older Americans to retire with a guaranteed monthly check. But retirees are not the only beneficiaries. Social Security has also helped disabled workers and children who have lost a parent by paying out benefits to help ease their financial burdens.

As described in Chapter 3, the program has its own dedicated funding stream through FICA taxes (employees currently pay 6.2 percent of their revenue up to $102,000 and employers match the 6.2 percent). To be clear, the money that current workers are now paying into the system is not being held in a savings account until they need their benefits. Rather, this money is used to pay benefits to today's retirees and other program recipients. It is expected that future workers will provide the tax revenue to pay the Social Security benefits for today's workers when they are entitled to receive them. This system of financing Social Security benefits works fine as long as enough money comes into the system to pay out the benefits. But, as the median age of the U.S. population continues to rise, there will be fewer workers contributing to the Social Security program per retiree. For this reason, there is a very serious question about the long-term viability of the program. This is discussed further in this chapter.

From 1976 to 1982, Social Security operated at a deficit. That is, more was being issued out in benefits than was being brought in through FICA taxes. Faced with the impending collapse of Social Security, President Reagan and a Democratic Congress came together and raised the FICA payroll tax by two

---

[1] For more information about the history of Social Security, visit the Social Security Administration website at "http://www.ssa.gov/history/pdf/2007historybooklet.pdf".

percent. Not only did this change allow the program to generate enough revenue
to pay benefits, but it created significant surpluses in the Social Security program.
(i.e., more is collected in Social Security taxes than is paid out in benefits).
Currently the program is very well funded. In 2007, the federal government
collected almost $190 billion more than it paid out. Figure 13-1 illustrates the
annual surplus government revenue from Social Security from 1983 to 2007.

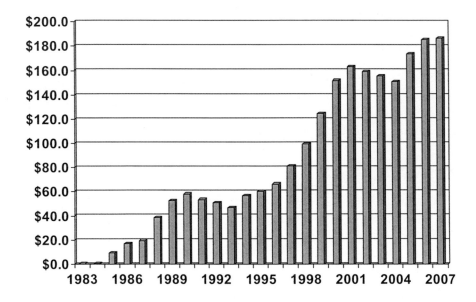

Figure 13-1. Social Security Surpluses (1983-2007)[2]

Figure 13-1 should be comforting as it would appear that the Social Security
program is flush full of cash – but it is not. The money that is collected by the
government for Social Security is dedicated to the program by law. Technically, it
cannot be spent on other government business; however, it is being spent on other
day-to-day government operations in a round-about way.

Surplus FICA taxes that are dedicated to Social Security go into two trust
funds: (1) the Old-Age and Survivors Insurance (OASI) Trust Fund, which is used
to pay retiree and survivor benefits; and (2) the Disability Insurance Trust Fund,
which pays disability benefits. But the Trust Funds are nothing more than

---

[2] Historical Social Security surplus figures can be found at the Congressional Budget Office at
   "http://www.cbo.gov/showdoc.cfm?index=1821&sequence=0".

accounting artifacts used to keep track of the amount of excess money collected. The money is not sitting in an account just waiting to be paid out to beneficiaries. Rather, in its infinite wisdom, the government takes the excess money and purchases U.S. Treasury securities. The excess FICA tax revenue is turned into cash that the government spends, and the Trust Fund is left holding U.S. Treasury bonds that promise to pay back the principal plus interest at some later date. Thus, the government is writing IOU's to itself in what amounts to an enormous shell game. Since the money is essentially being loaned to the U.S. government, it becomes part of the intragovernmental holdings that make up a sizeable portion of the national debt (see Chapter 6). Currently the two Social Security Trust Funds are holding a combined $2 trillion in U.S. Treasury securities. This accounts for about 21 percent of the total U.S. national debt.

What should concern all Americans is the fact that the SSA projects that in 2017 the program will no longer generate a surplus. At that point, the government will be required to dip into the funds that are technically in the Trust accounts to make benefit payment. This will immediately cause two major problems. First, the government will no longer have the tax revenue produced by excess FICA tax collections that it has grown accustomed to spending as part of its normal annual operating capital. Without the expected Social Security surplus funds for this year, the nation's current projected budget deficit would be far higher than "just" $400 billion; it would be closer to $600 billion.

The second major issue – and the more important issue – is, where will the government find the money to repay the Trust funds? Again, the $2 trillion owed back to the Social Security Trusts has already been spent. After 2017, not only will the government no longer have the revenues generated by the Social Security surplus to spend, but the government will have to commit money to pay back the SSA in order to allow Social Security benefits to be paid without interruption. The debt owed to the SSA is backed up by the full faith and credit of the United States government, and the federal government has never defaulted on a loan. However, that does not change the fact that there is no account which can be tapped, nor is there any real source of new income that will be able to cover the $2 trillion. As such, it is likely that the government will be forced to raise taxes, borrow even more money from the public, and reduce benefits. Obviously, none of these options are desirable – but they will be necessary.

As citizens, we should be concerned about the viability of the Social Security system and look to politicians in Washington to address the growing financial issue. At a minimum, the government should start to weigh options and take actions in order to prepare to repay the Social Security Trusts. However, even if the government finds a way to pay back the money that it owes, the SSA projects that the Trust Funds will be completely depleted by 2041. This may seem a long way off, but the longer the nation waits to address the problems, the more costly and painful it will be to maintain Social Security (assuming Americans want to maintain the system). The only thing that is clear is that if no changes are made to the program it will fail.

Chapter 14

DISCUSSION: WHERE THE U.S. IS NOW AND PRIORITIES FOR THE FUTURE

There are normal economic cycles, and looking back over the financial figures during the last five presidencies, we can find high points and low points. That said, Presidents and Congress are not helpless bystanders hoping for prosperous economic times. They have the power to impact the economy through public policies. Government actions can soften economic hardships during downturns and keep the economy from overheating when GDP is rising. We should expect our government to take appropriate actions, and through elections we must hold our elected representatives responsible.

As we come to the end of the current Bush presidency, Americans should be concerned about the economic condition and financial stability of the nation. The 1990s saw significant improvement of many of the key fiscal measures discussed in this book, but changes in U.S. economic policies in the 2000s have reversed those improvements. The rapidly rising economy, rising tax revenues, modest spending increases, budget surpluses, low unemployment, and tame inflation that Americans enjoyed a decade ago are nothing more than rapidly fading memories.

On virtually every major economic factor, the U.S. economy is worsening and we are now in the midst of a serious and debilitating global credit crisis. Even more unsettling is the fact that we do not know where the bottom actually is. As bad as things are, they could very well get much worse. Toward this end, most of the financial numbers discussed in the book only include figures through 2007. If we just look at the 2008 figures that are available, we see a nation that is sinking into even greater financial trouble. The economy is slowing and is likely already in recession. With fluctuating energy costs and rising commodities prices, inflation is increasing faster than at any point in the last three decades. Housing foreclosures are reaching record levels and unemployment is ticking up. The budget deficit is rising as government spending increases and tax receipts fall. With all of the taxpayer bailouts for financial firms, the budget deficit for next year is projected to be as high as $1 trillion. The national debt continues to grow at an unsustainable level, and foreigners are accumulating that debt faster than ever before. The trade deficit continues to hover near an all-time high. Clearly, there are many reasons to be pessimistic.

To begin to solve these problems, government leaders and policy makers need to understand what each of the numbers mean and how they are inter-related. Working to improve one number will have effects on other numbers. Some of the inter-relationships are more obvious than others, such as the fact that the annual budget deficits add up to make up the total national debt. Thus, before the national debt can be reduced, deficit spending must not only end, but budget surpluses must be created that can be applied toward paying down the debt. Another simple example is that when the economy slows, tax revenues tend to shrink which negatively impacts the budget. Other relationships are not necessarily as clear, such as how the value of the dollar and interest rates are impacted by government policies. Deficit spending and unsustainable debt accumulation send a message to international bankers that the U.S. is not serious about fiscal policies and maintaining the value of the dollar. When the national debt grows unusually high relative to the GDP (as it has in recent years), foreign investors begin to worry that the U.S. will begin printing more money to make payments. At some point, this devalues the dollar and investors expect a higher return (i.e., higher interest rates) to hedge against depreciation of their investments. Thus, it becomes more expensive to finance the debt.

In addition, as the dollar falls, there are many different impacts that affect the U.S. current account. With a falling dollar, U.S.-made products become cheaper around the globe. This usually results in increasing U.S. exports which would improve the U.S. current account. However, when the dollar is weak, foreigners also tend to buy U.S. assets (i.e., companies, property, equipment) at a cheaper price, which is obviously undesirable. New infusions of foreign debt capital through the sale of U.S. Treasury securities may be necessary for the U.S. to finance its overall national debt. Again, this may require higher interest rates in order to entice and secure foreign investment. As this happens, there is a greater outflow of cash in the form of interest payments, which has a negative effect on the U.S. current account. So while a falling dollar can help reduce the trade deficit, it also leads to foreign purchases of U.S. assets and higher interest payments on the national debt. These types of contradictions can confuse voters and allow incumbent politicians to spin their records by "cherry picking" the numbers they want to highlight. This is why it is important to understand all of the numbers and how they correlate with each other.

Make no mistake, a strong dollar is preferable to a weak dollar, and the fact is that the fiscal policies of our government have put the dollar at risk against other major currencies. The falling dollar contributed to rising oil prices. Oil is a global commodity that is bought and sold around the world in dollars, and with a devalued dollar, oil producers expected more dollars. The weak dollar has allowed firms in other nations to take advantage of favorable exchange rates to purchase American assets at bargain prices in this country. It is not surprising that we see foreign firms and sovereign wealth funds buying up landmark buildings in New York. No one should have been shocked to see InBev, the Belgian-based multi-national beverage firm, successfully buy out Anheuser-Busch – the iconic American beer company. The Indiana Toll Road is now being leased to a Spanish firm for the next 75 years (for a total $3.8 billion). These are just a few examples, but when the dollar was stronger, these transactions simply would not have taken place. With the weaker dollar, American assets have become affordable, and even cheap. Such purchases are happening all around us and with greater frequency.

One segment of the economy that foreigners are gaining control of that could prove damaging for Americans is the nation's financial institutions. The housing and credit collapse has sent commercial and investment banks scrambling for cash. As a result, billions of dollars in foreign-owned cash have flowed into U.S. commercial banks, Wall Street investment firms, and even mortgage lending institutions such as Freddie Mac and Fannie Mae. With foreigners now holding large equity (ownership) stakes in the largest American financial firms, virtually every American who has a loan for personal property (house, car, boat, etc.) or a mutual fund or stock account with an investment firm now owes money in some way to foreign creditors. This has further facilitated the transfer of wealth away from the U.S. and has put America's sovereignty in jeopardy.

CAPITALISM AND THE SHIFTING ECONOMIC WORLD

Many of the problems that we are facing today can be traced to a basic ignorance of capitalism and the changes that are happening in the global economy. There seems to be an adherence to the mythic belief that the U.S. is the greatest economic power in the world and it always will be. The former is true for the time being, but the latter is certainly debatable. The future is uncertain, but what is certain is that other nations are seeing tremendous growth in their economies. If history has taught us anything it is that empires and great powers rise and fall. There is no guarantee that the U.S. will remain the world's greatest economic power. Yet, this belief is held by many and it is perpetuated (falsely) by the public policies chosen by our leaders in Washington. The out-of-control spending is more fitting for an economy that is growing rapidly, than for one that is slowing and which is already burdened with tremendous debt.

Capital will always flow to the most efficient markets. That is, capital will be invested where goods and services can be produced with the greatest profit margins. There is no place for national identity or borders within capitalism. As trade barriers have fallen and communications technologies have improved, the world has grown smaller and capital has flowed across the globe. We see the effects of global capitalism playing out all around us. Jobs are being outsourced and foreign firms are buying America's most-recognized companies. American corporations were once revered around the world, but are increasingly struggling to compete against well-financed and rapidly improving firms in foreign markets.

As described above, and in Chapter 8, we are in the midst of a period of rapid outflow of American wealth to other nations. Americans need to accept that the world is catching up to the U.S., and in some economic sectors foreign nations have surpassed the U.S. Too many Americans do not fully appreciate what this means. Many hold on to the notion that U.S. workers and U.S. firms are just better than their foreign counterparts. However, the growing power of foreign economies and foreign firms tells a very different story.

One indicator of the impact of the shifting global landscape on U.S. competitiveness is that in the past, the best and brightest students from around the world came to the U.S. to earn college and graduate degrees. They then stayed in the country because the best job opportunities and standards of living were here in America. The net inflow of human capital fostered the spirit of American entrepreneurship, innovation, and ingenuity. But this is no longer the case. Great and growing opportunities and rising standards of living are commonplace around the world.

Most Americans are well aware of the blue-collar manufacturing jobs that have moved out of the U.S. and across the globe. However, what should be more alarming is that the next wave of great innovations in information technology or biotechnology is just as likely, if not more likely, to come from India as it is to come from the U.S. A Japanese firm may be the one that develops and patents a nanotechnology advance that radically alters the electronics industry. Europeans may come up with the next great green energy solution that shifts the world from fossil fuels to an alternative, clean and renewable energy. This would have been far less likely 25 years ago, but today it is a reality of the global economy.

Quite frankly, there has to be a major shift in thinking in Washington. Our leaders need to better understand the growing problems themselves, and then they need to lead and tell the American people the truth. For decades the U.S. has been the undisputed economic superpower in the world, but this is changing. Our public policies need to reflect the realities of the global economy or we will not be able to compete effectively. It requires a dose of economic reality and discipline that has been sadly missing in Washington.

THE NEED FOR FISCAL DISCIPLINE

Many of the problems that the nation is now facing are long-term problems that have been exacerbated by the recent explosion in government spending combined with tax cuts. We cannot have our cake and eat it too. At a minimum, the government has to work to balance the federal budget. Every program and every federal agency should be scrutinized. It goes without saying that waste, fraud, and abuse must be eliminated, but that is not enough. The looming and growing financial burdens of the national debt and programs such as Social Security require careful evaluation of all government programs and spending priorities. Any programs that cannot demonstrate clear value for American people – value that far exceeds the amount spent on the program – should be eliminated.

In addition, the use of supplemental spending bills to fund the wars in Iraq and Afghanistan has to end immediately. Supplemental spending bills fall outside of the normal budget process and should only be used for emergencies. The bulk of war costs should be added into the federal budget so that it can be scrutinized and audited in a manner consistent with other normal annual government expenditures. Tens of billions of dollars that have been committed to fighting in Iraq and Afghanistan have been lost, pilfered, wasted, or are otherwise unaccounted for. This would be far less likely if Congress required the President to include his projected war costs in the annual budget.

Finally, targeted earmarks that are kept hidden from public scrutiny and which often only benefit narrow special interests must be stricken from spending bills. But, diligence on the part of the government to eliminate earmarks, useless programs, war profiteering, and general mismanagement of funds, is likely to only cut tens of billions to perhaps a few hundred billion dollars from the budget. This would be a good start, but much more has to be done to balance federal budgets. Nothing should be off the table including raising taxes, slowing increases to large entitlement programs such as Medicare and Social Security, and freezing budgets for federal agencies. Any solution will likely require a combination of strategies to address the growing fiscal crisis.

At a more fundamental level, the American people have to carefully consider the meanings of fiscal discipline and sound economic policy. Fiscal discipline does not simply mean cutting taxes. Certainly, cutting taxes can boost business spending, which can spur the economy, but there is a point at which taxes can become too low to cover the spending priorities of the American people. At the other extreme, if taxes are too high it can stunt the economy and prevent technological innovations. The problem is that the equilibrium point is not fixed; it fluctuates with the normal economic cycle. The end result is that there are times to raise taxes and there are times to cut taxes. When new priorities require federal resources to be expended, such as the rebuilding of the Gulf Coast after Hurricane Katrina or going to war in Afghanistan after 9/11, taxes should be raised to cover these expenses. When the economy goes into recession, or the government generates significant excess tax revenues, serious consideration should be given to tax cuts and/or rebates.

With respect to debt, it can be an important part of a disciplined and responsible economic policy. Debt, in and of itself, is not necessarily a bad thing and there are times when deficit spending is appropriate; however, it must be for a limited time and it should offer a clear, long-term benefit for the American people. Consider a high school graduate who goes on to college to earn a degree. That student may accumulate a fair amount of debt during his/her college years, but upon graduation the student's investment in developing skills and knowledge should open up new opportunities that yield higher paying jobs. The student must then pay back the debt and as long as the investment results in a high enough paying job to pay back the loan and still earn a living, it would be a valuable and worthwhile investment. Obviously, the key to successful deficit spending is that it is temporary and limited by the future value of the investment that one is spending borrowed money on. This is the lesson that many politicians have not learned, otherwise the federal government would not engage in the structural deficit spending and borrowing practices that it has engaged in year after year.

Fiscal discipline is not a partisan issue. Both Republicans and Democrats should consider the fiscal implications of their priorities before promoting them. President Reagan is remembered for his sweeping tax cuts, but the reality is that when the federal deficits exploded and Social Security was on the verge of collapse, he worked with Congress to implement significant tax increases. Most notably, Social Security was not only saved, but it began to generate significant tax surpluses that will pay for the program for decades. This was a good example of fiscal discipline and sound economic policy.

On the other side of the political spectrum, the 1993 tax increase pushed by President Clinton and his White House just squeaked through Congress (Vice President Al Gore had to cast the deciding vote in the Senate to break a tie), but it generated new revenues for the federal government that improved the budget situation of the federal government every year of the Clinton presidency. In his final year in office, the federal government generated a record surplus of $236 billion and was actually paying down the principal of the national debt. Fiscal discipline in Washington is not an oxymoron and it can be done. But it requires political will and commitment.

We are now seeing the myriad of problems that occur when taxes are cut but spending increases to the point of creating record deficits. Discipline and sound fiscal policy occurs when there is a balance between the spending priorities of the nation and the tax policies used to generate government revenues. If we, as citizens, want good schools, or better roads and bridges, or universal health care; if we believe that prosecuting a war on global terrorism and occupying Iraq are noble causes; if we want to prevent the spread of AIDS or help end global hunger and poverty; then we have to be willing to make the sacrifices to pay for these endeavors. We certainly should not be continuously borrowing money from foreign countries and passing the costs to future generations of Americans if they are such important priorities.

BROAD FISCAL POLICY RECOMMENDATIONS

There are no magic solutions to the growing fiscal challenges, it just requires leadership and shared sacrifice. Without going into too much detail, this section outlines some of the economic policy goals that should be pursued by the federal government. How the government achieves these goals is left up to politicians and public policy experts.

The most pressing issue is that the federal government must balance its budget and has to stop borrowing money. To do this, the government needs to slow the rate of spending, if not cut spending, and raise taxes in order to balance annual spending (including supplemental spending bills) with annual tax revenues. The 2008 deficit was $440 billion, and next year it will likely be at least twice as large. Finding ways to close the gap is a major challenge, and it will likely take years to get there.

On top of closing the budget gap, the government has to stop using Social Security surplus tax revenues (almost $200 billion for this year) as part of its operational revenues. We know that in less than a decade FICA taxes for the

Social Security program will no longer generate surplus revenues and the government will have to begin repaying the Social Security Trusts the $2 trillion that it owes. The government should begin to wean itself off of the Social Security surplus now, and it should set the surplus money aside. It would be wise to invest a portion of the money into a mix of private and foreign held interest bearing accounts. This would allow the Social Security Trusts to hold diversified investment vehicles and reduce the amount the federal government will be required to pay back. It could also help to shore up faltering American financial institutions that are being forced to secure foreign investment to avoid going into bankruptcy.

Any surplus Social Security tax revenue that is converted into U.S. Treasury securities should not be spent on new federal programs, or even current federal programs. Instead, surplus revenues would be better utilized if they were used to pay down the national debt, particularly to foreign-holders of U.S. debt. To prevent undue outside influence on American interests, and to maintain a clear sense of national sovereignty, we need to reduce the amount of money owed to foreigners.

Ultimately, government solutions to the fiscal challenges facing the nation will create a more favorable climate for the private sector. Fiscal discipline demonstrated by a balanced budget and reduction of the national debt would send an unambiguous signal to the country and the rest of the world that the U.S. government is serious about managing its finances. This would stabilize the dollar which would help tamp down rising global food and oil prices and allow U.S. firms to purchase foreign assets at a better exchange rate. As energy and food prices dropped, the U.S. economy would improve as American consumers would have more disposable income to spend on goods and services. This would obviously help publicly-traded companies on the U.S. stock markets, as they would achieve higher sales and profit figures. This additional capital could be used to expand and invest in new markets around the world. It would also help to prevent foreigners from purchasing controlling interest in U.S. firms and acquiring American assets by making them more expensive in the global market.

There are cascading benefits to improving U.S. government fiscal policies. But, obviously, the devil is in the details. Choosing the spending priorities is not easy. What would a single-payer universal health care program cost? Should defense spending be cut? How much money should be committed to environmental causes? Do we need to increase or decrease funding for education programs? On the tax side, who should be taxed? Are there products that should be taxed at a higher rate? How much additional tax revenue is needed and for how long? These are vexing questions that must be answered because the federal government has limited resources. They require careful consideration and actions on the part of the President and the Congress. We need our politicians to lead and to make the tough choices we elect them to make. If they do not or will not, or they make the wrong choices that lead to even poorer fiscal performance, voters must hold them accountable and vote them out. Americans simply cannot afford to wait any longer to see action.

Chapter 15

CONCLUDING THOUGHTS

There are significant challenges facing the nation – the global credit crisis, the ongoing war on terror, fluctuating oil prices, rising costs of health care, global warming, a crumbling infrastructure, etc. – but none of these are as challenging as the worsening economic condition of the country. The reason is that all public policies and government initiatives are impacted by the economy. Without resources and money, options to address any other challenge are limited.

We now live in a truly global economy and American firms must compete in that arena. The top competitor may not be located just down the street, but half a world away. In recent years, there has been rapid shift in the wealth of nations. The U.S. has gone from the greatest creditor nation in the world, to its largest debtor nation over the course of several decades. This is one of the results of the steady decline in the fiscal performance of the federal government.

As shown in the figures provided in this book, there is plenty of blame to go around. Presidents from both political parties have held office and both Houses of Congress have been controlled by Democrats and Republicans at various times during the last 30 years. There have been ups and downs during the presidential terms of all of the last five Presidents, but the bottom line is that the economic problems facing the nation have grown. Rather than try to assign blame, it is better to now recognize that the financial outlooks for the U.S. for both the near term (next five years) and the longer term are not encouraging. Recognizing this to be true, and understanding how and why it has happened, is the first step to solving the problem. Only then can economic proposals that change the fiscal fortunes of the nation emerge.

Serious leaders must now brace the country for real economic sacrifice. Americans have elected leaders who have spent far beyond the nation's means, and have financed the deficit spending through debt – increasingly owed to foreigners. Unfortunately, the hyper-partisan nature of politics in Washington DC makes it even more difficult to agree on solutions that can address the problems. Vitriolic debate and the constant spin in an effort to score political points add another layer of difficulty to the implementation of reasonable solutions. The result is that politicians bicker about small matters, while all the while the macro-level economic figures worsen.

The primary goal of this book was to provide an honest and unbiased look at the financial performance of the government over the last 30 years. With this knowledge, policy makers, analysts, and students of government can see where the nation now stands and the major fiscal challenges facing the nation. Ultimately, we have a choice. We can allow the nation to sink further into the fiscal morass it finds itself in, or through a shared sense of sacrifice and commitment to turn the fortunes of the nation around, we can face the challenges head on. Much work needs to be done and now more than ever, we need bold leadership in Washington that is willing to be honest with the American people, make tough economic decisions, and which offers innovative government solutions. Without significant changes in U.S. economic policies, and a more engaged populace to hold politicians responsible, we should not expect any change in the fiscal fortunes of the nation and the U.S. will find itself struggling to compete in the global economy.

INDEX